Standing on the Promises

By Beverly Daniel

Table of Contents

ACKNOWLEDGEMENTS

I could not have written this book without the help of several people. Thanks to the wonderful team of people at The Book Publishing Pros, especially Nick Wilson. Thanks to my husband, Mark Daniel, for his love and support. Thanks to my sister-in-law, Cindy Daniel, for her technical help. Thanks to my cousin, Brenda Yoakum Burks, for sharing her memories of growing up in Rockdale. And most of all, thanks to Jesus Christ for inspiring me to write this book and guiding me through the journey.

DEDICATION

This book is dedicated to my mother, Mary Virginia Layne Yoakum, whose stories of growing up in Texas during the Great Depression inspired me to write this book.

CHAPTER 1

THE STAINED GLASS WINDOW

The sunlight pouring through the new stained glass window never failed to fill Laura Patterson with joy and inspiration as she and her husband Sam sat every Sunday morning, without fail, on the third pew, "congregation right", of the Sandy Creek Methodist Church.

Not only the beautiful stained glass window but the new wine-colored velvet pew cushions and the new hymnals, as well, were courtesy of Miss Helen, who, at the ripe old age of 95, had passed away, leaving her entire fortune (with the exception of the farm itself) to her church. Some who knew Miss Helen whispered their shock that she would leave the church anything, as she refused to tithe and acted as though her presence alone was gift enough. Others said they weren't surprised at the huge amount because she had four cents of every nickel she ever made and must have finally figured out she couldn't take it with her.

There were even those who suggested that she felt guilty at the end for being such a tightwad and hoped to bribe her way into a heaven she wasn't all that sure she was welcome in. The kinder-thinking folks said that maybe Miss Helen had been saving up for just the right time to bless her church family with this wonderful gift after she was dead and no longer around to be thanked. The pastor was a proponent of this theory, but even his wife was doubtful.

Laura, who had known Miss Helen her entire life, felt that all the theories had merit except for the kinder one. That one was a real reach. Being the closest living relative of the grumpy old maid,

Laura knew that if there had been any way Miss Helen could have taken it all with her, she would have, and even then, it wouldn't have been enough to satisfy her. That she had actually left her fortune to their church still amazed her. Her husband Sam jokingly suggested they check the lining of the coffin, just in case.

.   None of this, however, kept Laura from enjoying the wonderful improvements to their church, particularly that beautiful stained glass window that featured a white-robed Jesus ascending into heaven yet looking right at you with a loving smile and palms out as if welcoming you to come along on the trip. When Miss Helen's will was read, Laura could not help but giggle just a little at the instructions, Helen left:

> I want a huge stained glass window, fifteen feet tall and six feet wide in a long oval but flat at the bottom like you see in churches in the city. I want it placed in the back wall behind the pulpit so that when the sun shines in, it illuminates the altar area.
>
> (And no, Pastor Chris, we do _not_ need a baptistry. That is for the Baptists. We Methodists only need to sprinkle.) I want the window to feature Jesus's entire body completely clothed in a white robe. He should have a gentle, sweet smile on his face, and under no circumstances should he be hanging on the cross, almost naked, suffering in agony like those Catholics like to show. (They don't seem to realize that HE IS RISEN) And I want Jesus and ONLY Jesus…. none of that

Virgin Mary holding his dead body stuff. I am
sure she was a fine person, but I don't want
her stealing Jesus's thunder. If you can't do
it the way I want, then don't do it at all.

Miss Helen was anything but subtle. She didn't much like their latest
minister, Pastor Chris, because he brought some new-fangled ideas
that, quite frankly, sounded more Baptist than Methodist. She felt
sure John Wesley would agree with her. No one knew where or
when she had ever visited a Baptist or Catholic church or why she
held them in such contempt, but they never dared ask for fear of
receiving one of her lectures about what was right about the
Methodists and wrong about everyone else.

When Laura was a little girl and had come to visit her Great-Aunt
Helen, she had received such a lecture. She had accompanied Miss
Helen on a visit to the new neighbors who had just moved into the
nearest farm around two miles down the dusty, winding road. No
word yet whether or not they were Methodists, but Miss Helen held
out hope and wanted to be the first to welcome them, lest those
Baptists or Catholics got a jump on her.

When the neighbors invited them in, Laura noticed a painting on the
wall of the Virgin Mary with a burning heart circled by thorns next
to one of Jesus wearing a painful crown of thorns with sweat and
blood pouring down His agonized face. His face looked upward,
His eyes reflecting great suffering as He hung on the cross. Oh, no!
thought Laura, Miss Helen will have a hissy fit over this!

Then, to make things matters worse, there was a priest there
squirting water (Holy water, Laura later learned) all over the walls
while muttering words Laura did not understand. When he finished,
he removed his priest's robe, patted the new neighbor on the back
and said, "Well, Max, how about a beer!"

Miss Helen, wide-eyed, pale with pursed lips, grabbed Laura's hand tightly. Laura just knew Miss Helen would turn into a pillar of salt or burst into flames. Instead, wide-eyed and completely speechless, Miss Helen turned and fled, still holding Laura's hand tightly. That was the one and only time Miss Helen was struck mute. God knew what he was doing.

Miss Helen didn't utter a single word until they arrived back home, then she got on her knees and prayed, making sure to mention the new neighbors, not so much to bless them, as to make sure God had witnessed the sheer horror that had transpired in that house. She then suggested they go straight to bed, and it was the next day, after Miss Helen had calmed down a bit, that Laura got her first lecture on the evils of the Catholic church and advised her to avoid "those people".

Laura made the mistake of responding, "But Miss Helen, in Sunday School, we learned that Jesus loves everyone and that we should love our neighbors as ourselves."

"Jesus never met a Catholic", said Miss Helen. Laura dared not mention that He had not ever met a Methodist, either, but she dared not risk Miss Helen's ire.

Noticing that Laura was lost in thought and had not heard Pastor Chris tell the congregation to stand for the first hymn, Sam gently nudged her. She was pleased they would be singing "Standing on the Promises", her favorite hymn.

CHAPTER 2

THE MOTHERLESS CHILD

"Standing, standing; standing on the promises of God, my Savior. Standing, standing, standing on the promises of God."

The hymn being sung by the congregation of the Sandy Creek Methodist Church floated on the breeze and reached nine-year-old Sara Jane Evans's open window less than a mile away. Sara couldn't always hear the music from the church, but on this particular Sunday morning, a soft spring breeze carried the notes more clearly than usual, as though they urgently wanted to be heard.

Sara Jane sat on the floor of her tiny bedroom, head lying on her folded arms which were draped over the open windowsill, as she contemplated the late spring flowers. The beautiful yellow daffodils, the first to announce the imminent arrival of spring, had given way to the late spring central Texas wildflowers that covered the landscape in brilliant blues, reds, yellows, oranges, and pinks.

Sara Jane hoped and prayed that the wildflowers would bring happiness this year. Spring had always been her favorite season, but last spring had brought with it sadness and tears for both Sara Jane and her stepfather, Howard Mills. Sara Jane's beloved mother, Mary, had passed away almost one year ago in April when the wildflowers were at their most beautiful. That, at least, was some comfort, but spring would never be the same without her mother.

Sara Jane's mother had given birth pre-maturely to a baby boy who died two hours later, her grief hastening her own death the following day. Sara Jane had picked bluebonnets, Indian paint brushes, and black-eyed Susan's, her mother's favorites, and put them in a water-filled mason jar on her mother's nightstand. Her mother's last words were, "Beautiful. So beautiful." Then she was gone.

Sara Jane thought her mother was referring to the flowers, but Pastor Tim said he felt sure she was seeing heaven. Sara Jane hoped so, for if anyone deserved to go to heaven, it was her sweet mother. Her stepfather, stone-faced and silent, merely turned and left the room, slamming the screen door of the tiny house sorely in need of repair.

When he returned several hours later, an almost empty whiskey bottle in his hand, he drunkenly announced, "We ain't gonna be goin' to church no more. If there really was a God, he wouldn't have let that innocent baby and your mother die like that." Sara admitted the thought had occurred to her as well, and she felt a wall encase her heart.

That was not the first time Sara Jane had seen Howard drunk, and it definitely would not be the last. Marrying her mother two years ago had both softened his heart and strengthened his resolve not to drink so much. He had gone on a couple of benders from time to time, but for the most part, he remained sober. As Sara Jane's mother had pointed out, "I don't expect him to be a perfect man, just a better one." And for a while, he had been.

Then the drought and dust storms hit, all the way from the plains of Oklahoma down through the top half of Texas, affecting even Milam County, where they lived on a small cotton farm, and everything changed. Howard worked hard to keep the farm going to provide for their family, but he was easily discouraged and used alcohol to deal with his frustration. One night, he got very drunk and turned mean. Sara Jane had never seen him this bad. She heard them arguing loudly in the kitchen, something they seldom did because her mother had a patient and loving heart.

Fear ran through Sara Jane as she heard a loud slap. Crawling under the covers, she held on to her beloved dog, Buddy, and covered her ears so she wouldn't have to listen. It was bad enough that he yelled at her mother but hitting her was almost unbearable. "Please, God," she prayed, "make him stop!"

The next morning, her mother, sporting a bruise on her face, said nothing as she calmly set the table for breakfast. Sara Jane just hung her head, ashamed that she had not helped her mother and angry at Howard's drunken violence. A sobered-up and quiet Howard joined them for breakfast, refusing to make eye contact. Then, putting on his hat, he headed out for morning chores without saying a word.

Finally, while clearing the dishes, Sara Jane's mother spoke. "He's sorry, you know. He didn't mean to be like that, but he was frustrated and scared we might lose the farm, and he turned to alcohol instead of prayer. We need to forgive him and pray for him."

"Still," said Sara Jane, "he shouldn't have hit you."

"He knows that, and he promises he will never do it again. He's a good man, Sara. He just forgets that sometimes."

Sara Jane was always amazed at her mother's strength and patience. She sometimes remembered what it was like "BH" ...Before Howard. She had flashes of memory of her father taking her fishing or swinging her in the old tire swing in the oak tree behind the house near the pond and peach orchard. Her father had built her a house in that tree, her own special place. Although in need of repair, like the house, it was still there, and Sara Jane retreated to it when she needed to be alone. The smell and feel of the tree house brought back comforting memories of her father.

She remembered that her father loved to hug her mother and often brought her bouquets of just-picked wildflowers and that her mother was always singing and joyful as she completed her chores around the house. It was her father who had given her Buddy as a puppy. Her mother had looked at the scruffy, brown and white puppy with one brown ear and said, "Well, look at that! He looks like God started to paint him brown but got distracted." They all laughed except Buddy, who wasn't amused.

Then, one day, Sara Jane's father did not come home, and the singing stopped. Pastor Tim had appeared at the door, hat in hand, and sat down with Sara Jane's mother at the kitchen table, already set with a supper that would never be eaten. She remembered hearing her mother crying, but she did not understand why until later. All Sara Jane knew was that her father had not come home for supper and that it made her mother sad.

Sara Jane's mother remained sad for a long time, and finally, she understood that her father would never be coming home for supper again. She didn't remember the funeral at all but vaguely recalled lots of people coming and going in the house, talking in whispers, her mother trying to be strong and not give in to her grief. But the grief could not be held back, and soon it spread to Sara Jane, who finally realized the finality of it all. She thought the world had ended, and for her, at least, the world as she knew it was gone forever.

"Why did God have to take him?" she asked through her tears. "Sara Jane,' replied her mother, "we must never question God's will. He has His reasons for all things, and the Bible says we must not lean on our own understanding but place our trust in Him. I loved your father very much, but he is gone now, and life is for the living. He would want us to get on with it." And despite their grief, they did.

CHAPTER 3

SOMEONE TO LEAN ON

Sam was happy to notice that even though Laura had been lost in thought, she at least had a smile on her face and was now singing along with the congregation. That had not been the case for several months.

"Standing on the promises of God." Those words held special meaning for both Sam and Laura. They had lost their first child just six months before, and Laura was still having difficulty dealing with the loss. They had looked forward to the birth with great anticipation, Sam building a wooden cradle and Laura knitting caps and booties. They had made it all the way to the delivery date, and everything looked fine. But the baby, a little girl, was stillborn, and grief washed over them like a tidal wave.

Adding to their sorrow, the doctor told them that the birth had caused internal damage to Laura, and it was not likely she would ever be able to conceive again. They were both devastated, and Laura had fallen into a depression from which Sam feared she would never recover. He would find her in the room they had designated for the nursery, quietly moving in the rocking chair, fingering the knitted caps and booties, tears silently trickling down her face. Sam had wanted to put them away, but he feared it would make things worse, and in time, Laura held them less and less, finally giving them away to charity.

Day by day, Laura grew stronger. Sam knew it was her faith that sustained her, and he thanked God for bringing his wife back to him. Seeing her in church that Sunday, deep in thought but with a smile on her face, gave him hope, and hearing her sing so earnestly lifted his spirits even more.

Sam smiled and took Laura's hand as the song ended, and they sat back on the beautiful new pew cushions. Laura smiled back at Sam and gave his hand a squeeze. How blessed she felt to have Sam as her husband! His patience and love never faltered, and even though she knew he grieved for their lost child as much as she did, he always remained strong so that she would have someone to lean on. But who was there for him when she was so lost in her own grief that she could not consider his? God thought Laura. Sam's faith was unshakeable, and she vowed to work harder to match his level of faith.

CHAPTER 4

A WIDENESS IN GOD'S MERCY

Sara Jane and her mother worked hard on the farm for almost a year after her father's death, assisted occasionally by their church family. But they had their own farms to care for and troubles of their own. Despite their help, things got bad, and Sara Jane overheard her always-positive mother praying for things to get better.

"Dear Lord, you have promised not to give us more than we can handle, but Lord, I don't know how much more I can take. When You took my husband, I accepted it as Your will and tried so hard to be strong for Sara Jane, but it hasn't rained in over two months, and if the cotton crops don't make, we won't be able to put food on the table and might lose the farm. Give me strength, oh Lord, to get through this, and walk with me, for I cannot do this without you. In Jesus's name, Amen."

Then, one day several weeks later, it rained. Sara Jane and her mother ran outside, holding hands, laughing, and joyfully dancing in the rain. They gave thanks to God for his mercy.

Sara Jane and her mother were at the feed store in Rockdale a few days later, buying a new sack of flour and other supplies and discussing the new dress her mother would make her from the floral fabric of the cotton sack. As they started loading the supplies in the old truck, a handsome stranger walked over to them. "Excuse me, ma'am," said the man, removing his hat and revealing a beautiful head of wavy, brown hair, "My name's Howard Mills. Can I help you load those supplies?"

Sara Jane never knew where he came from or why he was so eager to help them, but she suspected it was her mother's beautiful brown eyes that drew him to her. Her mother smiled at Howard, noticing his twinkling blue eyes and nice manners.

Six months later, they were married, and Howard came to live with them on the cotton farm. He was nice enough, Sara Jane guessed, although he never paid much attention to her or Buddy. But her mother started singing again, so Sara Jane decided that if Howard was good for her mother, then he would just have to do.

CHAPTER 5

BRINGING IN THE SHEAVES

As the second hymn wafted on the breeze to Sara Jane's windowsill, she recalled the first time Howard had attended church with them. The three of them had not held hands as they walked to church like they had when her father was alive. And Howard had not sung the hymns with gusto like her father had done. She could still hear her father singing so beautifully, "Bringing in the sheaves, bringing in the sheaves. Here we come rejoicing, bringing in the sheaves."

Sara Jane had no idea what a sheave was, but she was too embarrassed to ask lest she appear ignorant. She also did not know why everyone was so happy to be bringing them in. But she had been taught that people should always be grateful for whatever they had, so she decided that whatever sheaves were, it was good to be grateful for them, so she happily sang along with her mother and father.

Now, hearing that hymn again, she remembered that Howard had fidgeted in the pew, and although he stood up as the pastor instructed, he did not sing along. One day, when Sara Jane was helping her mother hang the wet clothes on the clothesline, she pointed this out to her. Her mother paused for a moment, then, in her usual calm manner, explained that it was OK that Howard was not like her father. Her father had been a wonderful man, but it wasn't fair to Howard to compare them. "You must try to find the good in Howard as I do," said her mother. "I don't know what we would have done if he had not come along when he did. I think God may have sent him to us."

Sara Jane tried really hard after that to see the good in Howard because her mother had asked her to and because she really did want to like him better. But so far, the only good things she could find about him were that he worked hard and made things easier on her mother and, oh, yes, he had nice hair.

One day, Sara Jane decided to try talking to Howard so he might warm up to her a little. She had finished her chores and was outside playing with Buddy when she spotted Howard walking up the path from the cotton fields toward the house. He paused a moment to pet Buddy, the first time he had ever done so. Sara made a mental note to add "Petted Buddy" to her short list of positive things she was compiling on Howard.

"Uh, Howard", Sara Jane began, "What's a sheave?'

"A what?" he asked.

"A sheave. Like in the hymn."

"How should I know? Ask your mother."

Then he walked into the house, calling her mother's name. Sara Jane sighed and continued playing with her dog. "Well," she said to Buddy, "that's one more thing to add to the negatives. At this rate, the positives will never catch up." Buddy ran to catch the ball she threw, barking as if in agreement.

CHAPTER 6

TEA PARTIES AND BIRTHDAYS

It was wash day, and Laura hummed as she took down the clean white sheets she had hung out that morning on the backyard clothesline. As she carefully folded the sheets and placed them in the basket, her old calico cat, Methuselah, lazily rubbed against Laura's ankles, purring loudly. Laura was thankful that the dust had not been too bad today. Some days, back in Fort Worth, the air was so cloudy with dust from the plains that they didn't bother to hang the sheets out.

Laura smiled to herself as she petted Methuselah and remembered the days when she was a child and made a playhouse out of the sheets hanging on the line. Her sister joined her in the playhouse for a tea party, along with Methuselah, their favorite dolls and the tiny China teacups, saucers, and teapot they had gotten the previous Christmas from Miss Helen. When her father got home from work, he heard them giggling and walked to the playhouse. Pulling back the sheets, he said, "What's this, a party?"

"Girls only!" said the girls, laughing.

Her father laughed and walked back to the house, a big grin on his face.

"Methuselah," said Laura, "That tea party was fifteen years ago, and you were several years old then. You are definitely living up to your name!" Methuselah purred even louder and fluffed up his tail as if to show his pride in accomplishing feline longevity.

It had been years since Laura had seen her family. Her sister had married and moved to Oklahoma years before. Their mother joined them after Laura and Sam married and moved to Dallas. Then, when the dust got so bad and no crops would grow, her sister, her brother-in-law, and her mother moved to California with hundreds of others seeking a better life. She never heard from her after that and had no idea how to reach her. Later, she got word that her mother had passed away from dust pneumonia, and her father…. Well, Laura had no idea where he was or if he was even alive. Her heart ached when she thought of them.

Miss Helen had been her only living relative, and she had passed away this past year, leaving her farm to her and Sam. Thank God for Sam, she thought. How she adored him!

As if on cue, Sam came up the path from the fields, a big smile on his face.

"Hey, there! Hold on and let me help you with that.", said Sam. He was holding a bouquet of wildflowers and bowed as he handed them to her. "Beautiful flowers for a beautiful lady!" Then he took the basket from Laura.

"For me?" asked Laura as Sam gave her a kiss on the cheek and led her into the house.

"Why are you so early?" Laura asked as she placed the flowers in a mason jar on the kitchen table.

"Well, believe it or not, the fields are plowed, the cows are fed, and I decided to come home early to spend time with my beautiful wife!"

He grabbed her around the waist and spun her around the room in a mock ballroom dance. Laura laughed as they danced.

"I'm getting dizzy, you silly man!" said Laura. Sam sat her down in a kitchen chair, and they continued to laugh until they were out of breath.

"I haven't started supper yet, but I made a dewberry pie. You can have a tiny piece while I finish the biscuits, but only a tiny one. I don't want you to spoil your appetite. And wash up first," said Laura, rising from her chair and putting on her apron.

"You forgot," said Sam.

"Forgot what?"

"Today's your birthday!"

"Oh my, I guess I did forget!" said Laura as she sat back down, cup towel in her hand. "I've had a lot on my mind."

"Well, I'm not surprised. I heard that people lose their memory as they get old, and you ARE twenty-five years old today!" said Sam, with a twinkle in his eye. "You know, I'm the luckiest guy in the world to have you as a wife. Even if you ARE an old hag!"

"Old hag, huh? Well, if I'm old, you must be ancient! Better put your teeth in, old man, before you eat that pie!" And she gave him a big hug before heading for the pie cooling on the windowsill. To her amazement, a big candle was standing right in the middle of the pie.

"How on earth did that candle get there?" asked Laura.

'Must have been the birthday fairy", said Sam with a smile. "Now we just need to light it." and he pulled out a match, lit the candle, and started singing Happy Birthday.

"Should I come in now?" asked a voice from outside.

"Perfect timing, Hank!" responded Sam.

Hank, the foreman of the farm, entered with a small black dog with a big red bow on its neck.

"What's this?" asked Laura.

"Your birthday present," said Sam. "Tom Smiley's cattle dog had puppies a few months ago. He can't use this one because there's something wrong with her vocal cords.She can't bark. Plus, one of her legs is crooked, causing her to limp. He was thinking of putting her down, but I asked if I could have her. I knew if anybody could love her, it was you. I named her Queenie."

Laura kneeled and picked up the small black dog, giving her a hug. "Welcome to your new home, Queenie," and Queenie's tail started wagging as she lovingly looked into the eyes of her new mother.

CHAPTER 7

THE GOOD, THE BAD, AND THE UGLY

When the last hymn was sung, and the church service ended, Sara Jane rose to take Buddy for a walk. She always felt better walking among the wildflowers, and Buddy was a wonderful companion.

As she left the house that Sunday morning, Sara Jane heard Howard loudly snoring. Howard's snoring was #8 on her list of things she did not like about him. She felt slightly ashamed knowing her mother would not approve of such a list but felt some comfort knowing her mother would never know.

Sara Jane had dutifully kept a list of things she liked about Howard while her mother was alive, but try as she might, the list remained quite short. Once, when he got dressed up to take them to a friend's wedding in Rockdale, Sara Jane had added the third and fourth positive things to her list: #3 Looks nice when cleaned up, and #4 Has good hair when washed.

She had yet to come up with a 5th, but her list of things she did NOT like had grown longer. His snoring was annoying, but it didn't even compare to several other things like "Never talks to me", "Gets drunk", "Sometimes stays gone all night" and the worst one, "Sometimes hits Mama". Sara's mother had said God sent Howard to them. Sara Jane secretly wished God would take him back.

Yes, a walk with Buddy in the wildflowers was just what she needed, and from the way Buddy was wagging his tail, it was just what he needed, too. They headed for the tree house where she and Buddy loved to go. After her mother died and Howard started drinking more heavily, Sara Jane had used the tree house more and more as a haven away from Howard, who never even knew the tree house existed.

She had started stowing away small items that were precious to her: a seashell from Galveston her father had given her, a silver cross necklace from her mother, her mother's sewing thimble, her father's old pocket knife, and the only photo she had of herself and her parents. It was the day she was christened, and the three of them were all dressed up in their very best clothes. Sara kept these items in an old sewing tin along with all the money she had ever gotten, eight nickels her mom and dad had given her on special occasions. She wanted all these precious items as far away from Howard as possible because they represented her life before he entered it, and she didn't want his presence tainting them.

The last item Sara had added to her stash was a dusty mason jar of peaches her mother had canned one summer for the coming winter. She planned to never eat them, for it was not the peaches themselves that she cherished, but the memories the peaches evoked.

Sara smiled as she remembered helping her mother pick the peaches. After weeks of drought, it had rained non-stop for two days, turning the soil from cracked and dried to mushy black loam. They laughed in the rain as they slogged through the mud to the orchard, throwing mud at one another and eating the unwashed peaches as juice ran down their chins. Sara's heart ached at the memory, and Buddy licked the single tear that rolled down her face.

"Let's go, Buddy," said Sara. "I want to pick some flowers for Mama, Daddy, and Little Jimmy."

Before she realized it, Sara Jane found herself at the church cemetery on the hill. The fragrant honeysuckle she had planted at the gravesites filled the air. She placed the bouquet of wildflowers on her mother's and father's graves and a smaller one on the tiny grave beside them. "Baby Boy Mills" was all the tiny wooden marker said. "I love you, little Jimmy", said Sara Jane. Howard had not wanted to name the baby, who had only lived a few precious hours, saying it would only make things worse. But Sara Jane, who could not think of anything worse than burying the baby without a name, had named him "Jimmy" after her beloved father, James.

On the back of the wooden cross, she had scratched "Jimmy", never fearing Howard's wrath if he saw it because he never visited the graves. Sara Jane made another mental note to add "Never visits Mama and Jimmy's graves" to the list of things she didn't like about Howard.

"I love you, Mama and Daddy. I miss you both so much. Mama, the wildflowers are in bloom now, all your favorites. Daddy, Buddy and I play in the treehouse you built us more and more, and I think of you every day. I get so lonely sometimes, but having Buddy helps a lot. I am trying to be good, Mama, and find the positive things about Howard. Mama, I heard your favorite hymn this morning. It felt like you and Daddy were sending me a special "hello". Well, I'm going now, I guess. Please say hello to Jesus and little Jimmy for me."

Suddenly a red cardinal landed on her mother's tombstone, and Sara Jane smiled, knowing her mother had sent it to comfort her.

As Sara Jane and Buddy were leaving the cemetery, Buddy started barking, and it seemed like he wanted to show her something. He was standing by a fairly recent mound of dirt she had not seen before. The tiny tombstone had an angel on it and read, "Emily Patterson, Born and Died, 11-15-1936. Safe in the arms of Jesus."

Seeing the tiny headstone marking the grave, Sara Jane burst into tears. Another baby was taken too soon! It was all too much. Buddy turned his head sideways, not understanding what was wrong. Sara Jane sat down on the ground and wept until it seemed there were no tears left. Buddy lay next to her and placed his head on her leg.

Why, thought Sara Jane, was life so cruel? Those two babies were innocent, yet their lives were taken before they even had a chance to live. Without the constant presence of her mother reminding her of God's love, Sara Jane grew angrier with God. Although she missed going to church, she decided that, like Howard, it was the right decision.

"Standing on the promises" thought Sara Jane. Her mother and father had stood on God's promises and look what happened to them!

Wiping her tears with the back of her hand, Sara Jane stood up and said, "Come on, Buddy; let's go home. Nothing but broken promises here." And she walked down the hill toward the tiny farmhouse, vowing to never cry again.

CHAPTER 8

RUNNING FROM THE FIRE

"Where the heck you been?" asked Howard as Sara Jane walked into the house.

"Nowhere," replied Sara Jane, startled. She had not expected him to be home. She gently pushed Buddy behind her with her foot. Howard was drunk again, and this looked like it was going to be a bad one.

"You're lyin'! You been to the cemetery again, ain't you? I told you before, they ain't comin' back! Visitin' those graves don't do nuthin' but get you all upset." Howard paused to take another drink from the almost empty whiskey bottle, then, in a quieter voice he said, "One year today they died. One year today." Then, getting up, he paused, turned, and stared at Sara Jane, growling: "Why couldn't it have been you!"

As he kicked the chair away, he stumbled, causing Buddy to bark. Noticing Buddy, Howard gave the little dog a kick, causing Buddy to yelp and whimper. Sara Jane bent down and cradled Buddy in her arms.

"Why do you have to be so mean? Buddy never hurt anyone!" cried Sara.

"I told you a dozen times to keep that mutt out of the house! A dog don't belong in the house and he sure don't belong on anyone's bed! If I catch him in this house one more time, it's the last time you'll ever see him!"

Sara Jane knew he meant it. They had had the discussion before, and Sara tried keeping him out of Howard's sight. She had started leaving him outside, but secretly letting him into her bedroom at night. She got up early each morning to let him out before making breakfast for Howard.

"I'm sorry, Howard. I won't let him in again. Come on, Buddy, let's go outside." And she opened the screen door to let him out. "I'll start supper now."

"I don't want any supper tonight. And don't go fixin' any for yourself, either. Get to bed now. That's your punishment."

"But it's still light outside, and..." SLAP! The pain and shock caused her eyes to sting with tears. "Don't you backtalk me! "Do what I tell you", and he staggered into his bedroom.

Sara Jane knew not to push Howard when he was drunk, so she went to her room. Under her breath, she repeated, "I won't cry, I won't cry, I won't cry." And she sat on the edge of her bed, trying her hardest not to. The slap had hurt a lot, but his words had wounded her even more deeply. "Why couldn't it have been you?" he had said. Sara sometimes wished it had been. The tears began in earnest, and exhausted, Sara fell asleep.

Later that night, Sara heard a noise and sat up. It was Howard, snoring loudly. Good, she thought. This meant he would sleep through the night, giving her time to do what she had to do. Sara Jane realized she had been asleep for a few hours because it was dark outside.

She sat silently on the bed for a while, then, with resolve, opened the screen door and whispered for Buddy to come in. "Be extra quiet now, Buddy. We got something we have to do. We can't stay here anymore. It's just gonna get worse. I won't let him hurt you anymore, Buddy. I don't know where we're goin', but anywhere is better than here."

She grabbed her rucksack and tiptoed to the kitchen, where she took some biscuits left over from breakfast, two apples, some cheese, some beef jerky, a coil of thin rope, a cup towel, and a small box of matches, which she set aside. She added a tin bowl, a tin cup, and a canteen, which she filled with water, and a small canvas emergency kit containing a roll of gauze bandaging, antiseptic, and a small pair of scissors. She put everything in her rucksack and carried it back to her bedroom, where she added a small quilt and a change of clothes.

Suddenly, she heard a crash. Howard was cursing and stumbling around his bedroom. "Quick!" whispered Sara, "Get under the bed!" She tossed the rucksack under the bed with Buddy and quickly crawled under the bedcovers, fully dressed. To her absolute horror, Howard started toward her room, drunkenly wobbling and carrying a lit kerosine lamp.

Sara Jane prayed silently. "Oh, dear God! Please don't let him hurt Buddy and me. Protect us!" She stayed as still as she could and pretended to be asleep. Howard continued walking to her bed, breathing heavily. Soon he was leaning over her. She could smell the whiskey on his breath. Drunkenly he whispered, "So like your mother." and pulled back her covers. Sara Jane froze, praying he would leave her alone, but when he put his hand on her leg, she screamed, "No! Leave me alone!" and jumped out of her bed.

Hearing her scream, Buddy ran from under the bed, hurling his body at Howard and biting him on the arm, refusing to let go. Startled, Howard yelled and stumbled backwards, flinging Buddy off and tripping on the rag rug in the doorway of the kitchen, then falling and hitting his head on the floor. The lamp shattered as it hit the floor and caught the rag rug on fire. Howard screamed as the flames caught his clothes on fire and spread across the floor toward the kitchen curtains and tablecloth. Buddy barked furiously. Terrified, Sara Jane grabbed her rucksack and her walking stick by the door, and she and Buddy ran out the front door, not daring to look back.

Sara Jane ran all the way around the back of the house and down the long path to the tree house. She helped Buddy up first, then climbed up after him., out of breath. Finally, looking back, Sara Jane saw the roof catch fire and knew the house was doomed. She watched in horror and fascination.

"I don't know what to do, Buddy. There's no one who can help. There's nobody at the church this time of night, and that's the closest telephone." Sara remembered that the nearest neighbors, who lived more than three miles away, were in Louisiana attending a family member's wedding. She knew that the pitiful buckets of water from the water pump would do nothing to help. She didn't know if Howard was alive or dead, and she wouldn't be able to save him, anyway. Nor did she know if she wanted to. God only knew what he would do to her and Buddy if he survived.

She watched the fire, which continued to burn, until the sun came up. "We have to go, Buddy, "said Sara Jane. "We can't be found here. They might think I pushed Howard and started the fire on purpose."

She grabbed her precious tin sewing box, put it in the rucksack, then paused as she looked at the jar of peaches. "Buddy, I'm gonna have to leave these here. The jar is too heavy and might break. Maybe we can come back and get them one day."

"God, I know I've been mad at you, but I really need you now. Please be with me and Buddy and guide us on our travels. In Jesus's name, Amen."

Then she carried the rucksack and walking stick down the ladder and came back for Buddy. They headed off, away from the house, not having any idea where they were going.

CHAPTER 9

DOWN BY THE RIVERSIDE

Scared but determined to get as far away from the house as possible, Sara Jane and Buddy walked toward the river. "Buddy, Daddy always told me that if you are hiking in the woods, keep the river or the road in sight so you don't get lost. Better for us to stay away from the road for now. So, we're gonna stay close to the river and follow it."

They walked for two hours, then the sun started getting higher in the sky, and exhausted, hungry, and thirsty, they stopped.

They walked closer to the riverbank and sat under the sycamore, pecan, and cottonwood trees that provided shade and would prevent them from being seen. Sara Jane opened the rucksack, pulled out the canteen and filled the bowl and cup. She gulped down the cool water while Buddy loudly lapped up his. Then she pulled out a biscuit, some cheese, and some beef jerky, sharing it with Buddy, who ate ravenously.

"I know, Buddy. I'm hungry, too. We didn't have supper last night or breakfast this morning. I'm so tired, Buddy. Let's spread out the blanket under the trees where it's cool and shady and take a nap while it's so hot."

Exhausted, they fell asleep.

Sara awoke suddenly to the sound of a twig snapping. Then someone said her name. She looked up, and to her absolute horror, saw Howard, his face and arms severely burned. He was missing his nose and one ear. She could smell his singed skin. He reached out to Sara Jane with a hand missing its fingers and said, "So like your mother." Sara Jane screamed and tried to pull away but could not move. Everything was in slow motion.

She screamed again, then heard Buddy whining, and felt him licking her face. She suddenly awoke and realized it had all been a terrible dream. She burst into tears, trembling and holding Buddy close. "Oh, Buddy! It was so horrible! It was so real! We need to get further down the river where Howard can't find us." She packed up their gear and they made their way further down the river.

CHAPTER 10

THE BEAUTIFUL RIVER

An hour later, Sara Jane spied a spot in a bend in the river where her family used to go. Underneath the beautiful, twisted limbs of a huge live oak tree was an old fishing shack with a torn screened-in porch. "Mr. Eddie's fishing cabin!" exclaimed Sara Jane. She dropped her gear, and she and Buddy ran to the shack, which had not been used in a long time. The door of the screened-in porch was hanging by one hinge, and the boards, although they creaked a little, were still intact. There was a small wooden pull wagon lying on its side.

She and Buddy made their way through an unlocked wooden door and into the cabin which contained a small wooden table with two rickety chairs and a metal cot with a thin mattress. There were some shelves on the walls that contained a few beat-up old pots and pans, a couple of plates and cups, a bowl, and some old cutlery. Another shelf held an old metal camping lantern and a small propane cook stove.

The small cabin was dusty and sported cobwebs and a few curious spiders in one of the corners, where, ironically, leaned a tattered old broom. There were two small windows strategically placed in the walls to get a cross breeze, essential in a Texas summer. One small windowpane was broken, but the rest were intact. Sara tugged on them and discovered they could be raised, if not all the way, at least enough to let in some air.

"Do you remember this cabin, Buddy? When Daddy was still alive, we used to come here and stay a few days a couple of times a year. This is Mr. Eddie's cabin, but he gave my daddy permission to use it whenever we wanted. Those were the best days ever! I hadn't thought about this place in years."

Buddy smiled and wagged his tail, sharing in Sara Jane's happy memory.

"We can stay here for a while. Let's get our gear in."

Sara unpacked some of their gear and poured both of them a drink of water, then suddenly jumped up and said, "Buddy! I almost forgot the best part."

She left the cabin, Buddy following along as usual, and walked down to the edge of the river where an old rope with a large knot in the bottom hung loosely from a large branch of the same huge oak tree that shaded the cabin. "Look, Buddy! Daddy made this for us. He would hold me and we would swing out over the river and drop in and make a huge splash. Mama was sitting on the gravel bar in the shallower part, and she would laugh and laugh while you barked and played. Daddy would threaten to make her jump, too, but she wouldn't have any part in that. I kinda thought you wanted to, though, Buddy. Did you?"

Buddy dutifully barked and wagged his tail, confirming her suspicion.

Sara Jane lay on the riverbank, soaking in the memories of how they swam, fished, and played in the river. They always cooked and ate the fish they caught, and it was delicious. She wondered if there was any fishing gear at the cabin and if she might be able to catch and cook some herself.

Before she realized it, the sun had started to set, and the light of a beautiful full moon and a sky full of sparkling stars signaled the sounds of the crickets, frogs, cicadas, and night birds: a delightful critter symphony. A light breeze kept the mosquitoes away, and the soft lapping of the river over the rocks was only interrupted by the "Hoot! Hoot!" of an owl responding to a softer "Hoot!" from somewhere on the other side of the river. Lightning bugs flitted in the air like tiny fairies greeting one another with even tinier lanterns.

Serenaded by the sweet night sounds, Sara Jane and Buddy fell peacefully asleep, his head resting on her leg.

CHAPTER 11

OH HAPPY DAY

When the sun shone on her face, Sara Jane awoke, confused, wondering where she was.

When she remembered, she smiled, feeling rested and at peace for the first time in months despite having slept outside. Realizing Buddy was gone, she called out to him and found him happily chasing a frog along the riverbed.

"Hey, Buddy! Did you catch anything?"

Buddy ignored her and continued to focus on the illusive frog. Sara Jane crossed over to where the rucksack lay, realizing she had never carried her gear into the cabin.

She set down the rucksack and walking stick in the small wagon on the porch, then went into the cabin to get the broom. Sara Jane first swept away the cobwebs and the tops of the table and chairs. She then swept the debris onto the screened porch and then outside.

Sara took two cloths she found in the cabin and walked down to the river to wet them.

She used one of them to wash her face, hands, and body and immediately felt refreshed. Buddy came bounding up to her, tongue hanging out and smiling.

"Havin' fun, Buddy? "

Buddy responded by wagging his tail.

"Let's go to the cabin and have something to eat, OK? I bet you're as hungry as I am."

Buddy dutifully followed her to the cabin, lying on the floor next to the table. Sara Jane pulled the remaining food out of the rucksack and set it on the small table. She poured herself and Buddy some water, then shared a biscuit and some cheese.

"It's so nice here, Buddy. I feel like Mama and Daddy are with us here. I hope we can stay here at least another day or so."

Buddy gave a short bark in agreement, then ran out the door and back down to the river.

Sara Jane decided to look around the outside of the cabin, where she noticed a closet attached to the back of the cabin. She gently pulled open the door, whose hinges squeaked loudly, indicating that it had not been opened in a long time. Inside the closet, she found two old fishing rods and a fishing tackle box filled with fishing lures, a knife, and a fish scraper. A hammer and a screwdriver lay on a shelf. She closed the door and walked a few feet, where she found a tall, skinny table with a removable tray on top. Sara Jane wasn't sure what it was, then realized it was a fish-cleaning station.

Sara Jane decided to join Buddy at the river. As she walked down the riverbank, she noticed a beautiful redbud tree she had not seen last night. What a beautiful color it was! Sara loved these redbuds but lamented the fact that they only bloomed for a couple of months each year. Oh, well, she thought. The crape myrtles will bloom when the redbuds are finished. God made us something beautiful to enjoy each season.

Sara Jane heard splashing and saw Buddy playing in the shallow part of the river near the sand and gravel bar. He proudly held a tiny fish in his mouth and ran to show it to her.

"Well, look at you, Buddy! You caught a fish. I'm so proud of you!"

Suddenly, the fish slipped out of Buddy's mouth and back into the water. Buddy bounded after it. Sara Jane laughed gleefully, her troubles gone from her mind for the moment. She looked around at the beautiful river and decided to go swimming. She stripped off her clothes, kept on her underwear, then plopped down in the shallow part near the sand and gravel bar. She happily splashed about, then moved out into the deeper part where she could immerse her entire body. It was absolute bliss! Sara felt a joy she had not felt since before her mother died.

Sara Jane was soon exhausted. Still happy, she lay on the sand and gravel bar to rest. Buddy joined her and lay beside her.

"Oh, Buddy! I wish we could stay here forever!" Buddy placed his head on her leg and sighed.

They fell asleep, content and peaceful. When they awoke, the sun was starting to set. They arose and started back to the cabin carrying Sara Jane's wet clothes. She stripped out of her underwear and put her wet clothing on the wooden pull wagon to dry, then went inside and changed into the only other clothing she had with her. She then pulled out what was left of the biscuits and cheese and shared it with Buddy.

"Buddy, we're almost out of food. We've still got the apples and some beef jerky, but we might have to try catching some fish."

As night fell, Sara Jane and Buddy walked outside to soak in the night sounds and look at the beautiful full moon and stars that were reflected in the water. They sat on the riverbank, listening to the soft lapping sound of the water and smiling at the lightning bugs signaling to one another. Such peace!

After a while, Sara spoke, "I guess we really should sleep indoors tonight, Buddy. It's probably safer." She and Buddy returned to the cabin. Sara Jane tugged open the windows as far as they would go, then lay her small quilt on top of the cot and lay down. Buddy lay down on the floor beside her. They were soon fast asleep.

CHAPTER 12

GONE FISHING

Sara Jane slept restlessly that night, troubled once again with nightmares about Howard. When she awoke, Buddy jumped up on the cot and licked her face, sensing her stress. Sara Jane hugged him and said, "Buddy; you are the best friend I ever had."

Sara Jane retrieved an apple and the last of the beef jerky, which she fed to Buddy.

"Buddy", said Sara Jane, " 'except for one apple, we are out of food. Let's try our hand at fishin'.'"

They walked around to the back of the cabin, where she had found the fishing gear in the closet. She selected the smaller of the fishing poles and placed a lure on the end of it. She carried a large pan with a lid in case she caught something and walked down to the river with a pole, pan, and walking stick.

Sara Jane knew from experience that early morning or late evening were the best times to fish. It was still early enough to possibly catch something. She and Buddy walked to the deeper part of the river, where there were more trees and brush. She knew fish loved hanging out in places like that, but she also knew to check for water moccasins that sometimes hung out there. She carefully poked around with her walking stick. Not seeing any snakes, she tossed the fishing pole line into the water.

Sara Jane and Buddy fished for over an hour, then Sara Jane decided to call it quits until later that evening when they would try again. Just as she rose, she felt a tug on the line, then another. Buddy started barking in excitement as Sara Jane pulled the fish onto the shore. It was a nice size fish, at least a couple of pounds, and she felt very proud. She struggled with removing the lure from the fish's mouth and getting it into the pan because it flopped around frantically. She cut her hand on the sharp fins.

"Lord, you say you help those who help themselves. Well, I'm trying my hardest here to get Buddy and me some food, but I can't do this by myself. Please help me. In Jesus's name. Amen."

The fish calmed down some, allowing Sara Jane to get it in the pan with the lid on, and she thanked God for His assistance. With a bleeding hand, Sara Jane carried the pot, walking stick and fishing pole back to the cabin. She poured water over her wound and applied an antiseptic and wrapped some bandage around it. She then retrieved the knife and fish scaler from the fishing tackle box and placed them, along with the fish, in the pan on the fish cleaning station. Buddy dutifully sat down near her.

"Lord," prayed Sara Jane. "I know you are with me 'cause you helped me calm the fish. I need you to help me clean this fish 'cause this is the part I hate the most. I watched Daddy, but I never done it myself."

She placed the fish on the tray, grabbed the knife, and, with some effort, managed to cut off the fish's head and tail, apologizing to the fish as she did it. She then scraped off as much as she could of the fish scales, sliced open the fish, and pulled out the fish guts with a large spoon. She asked God to keep her from getting sick to her stomach as she did this.

She placed the guts on the ground, telling Buddy he was welcome to eat them but secretly hoping he wouldn't. Buddy, hungry and having no shame, gobbled them up.

"Yuk!" said Sara Jane as she carried the fish into the cabin. She laid the fish on a plate and cut it into four large pieces, then placed the propane cook stove on the small table. She looked around and found a tiny bit of lard left in a can, which she placed in a frying pan on the cook stove. She turned on the tiny stove, grateful that a small flame had come on.

Once the lard was good and hot, Sara Jane carefully placed the fish in the pan with a fork, thanking her mother for teaching her how to cook. When the fish was fully cooked, she turned off the stove, removed the fish, and placed the pieces on a plate. It smelled wonderful! Sara Jane laughed as Buddy licked his lips.

"We gotta let it cool down first, Buddy. And we need to thank God for helping us."

When the fish had cooled down enough, Sara Jane sat down and gave thanks. She then broke off a piece of fish, making sure there were no bones in it, and gave it to Buddy. She eagerly ate one of the large pieces, telling Buddy they needed to save the rest for the next day.

After cleaning up the mess, Sara Jane and Buddy walked outside, sat on the riverbank, and watched the sun go down, Sara Jane's arm around Buddy.

"God is good," she said.

CHAPTER 13

SNAKES AND DEWBERRIES

Sara Jane and Buddy had more fish for breakfast, and she wrapped the remaining piece to have it later. She had hoped she and Buddy could stay longer, but she had another nightmare where Howard had found them and began to get anxious about staying longer. She packed up all her things and placed the rucksack into the small wooden pull wagon, leaving four of her nickels behind to help with the cost. Grabbing her walking stick, she and Buddy headed on down the way.

They had walked about half an hour when Sara Jane recognized some familiar bushes and vines.

"Look, Buddy, dewberries!"

Sara Jane took the bowl and cup and raced toward the bushes, feverishly picking the large purple berries and stuffing them in her mouth. She then started filling the bowl and cup with them. Her attention was broken by a dreaded sound. A rattlesnake shook its tail rattlers in warning, and Sara Jane realized she had been careless in her excitement and left her walking stick on the ground near her rucksack. She froze, and Buddy started furiously barking.

"Buddy," said Sara, slowly backing away from the snake, "stay still and stop barking."

But Buddy, determined to protect Sara Jane, charged the snake, which attempted to bury its poisonous fangs in his side. Buddy twisted away in time but lowered his head and charged again. The snake struck at Buddy again, this time biting him on the side of his face. Buddy yelped but managed to grab the snake by its neck, biting all the way through and killing the snake, whose body continued trembling a moment longer.

Sara Jane, familiar with the poisonous rattlesnake, knew their bite was sometimes fatal, depending on the size of the person or animal bitten and the amount of venom injected. She ran to Buddy and hugged him, tears pouring down her face.

"Oh, Buddy! This was my fault. I was careless, and now you're hurt."

Buddy had started whining as the painful venom flowed through his body. Sara Jane knew she had to get Buddy somewhere safe where she could keep him quiet and still. She removed the rucksack from the wagon and placed the small quilt in it. She then carefully and, with great difficulty, lifted Buddy into the wagon and admonished him to lie still. He was whining and exhausted, and Sara Jane could tell his face was starting to swell.

"Oh, Lord. I need you to help Buddy. I don't know how to live without him. I beg you to heal him and help me find a quiet, safe place where he can rest. In Jesus's name, Amen."

Sara Jane lifted the rucksack onto her back, grabbed her walking stick, and began pulling the wagon down the road.

CHAPTER 14

HIGHER GROUND

As Sara Jane pulled Buddy in the wagon, he continued softly whining in pain. Sara Jane's heart was breaking from the sound, which added to her guilt. After half an hour of pulling, she stopped to check on him and offer him water, which he refused. She took a drink and noticed a large white building in the distance.

As she pulled the wagon closer, she realized it was a large, two-story farmhouse with a wrap-around porch and gingerbread trim. The beautiful house featured blue shutters and a matching door. On the porch were two white rocking chairs. Hanging baskets of spring flowers hung from the porch eaves. Sara had not seen a house this beautiful since that large house in Rockdale she saw when she was younger.

The owner must have a green thumb because there was a beautiful flower bed along the white picket fence that surrounded the house. If Sara Jane could have designed her own house, it would look just like this.

Hiding behind a copse of trees, she looked around the grounds to make sure there were no people in sight.

The only person she saw was a woman in a straw hat working in her garden, her back turned away. Sara Jane realized that if she moved quickly, she could hide behind a nearby shed. Apologizing to

Buddy, she moved as quickly as she could, hoping the woman would not turn around.

Thankfully, the woman continued hoeing with her back turned. Sara Jane then saw there was a barn on the other side of the house and decided to seek shelter there. They had almost made it to the barn when a black dog came running toward them. Sara froze, fearing that the dog would bark and draw attention to them.

Oddly, the dog did not bark but ran to the wagon and sniffed Buddy instead. The dog then gently licked Buddy's bite wound.

Sara Jane spoke to the dog, saying, "Thank you, little dog, for not barking. This here's Buddy and he's hurt bad. I'm Sara Jane. I hope it's OK with you, but we need to hide in your barn for a few days." The dog made no sound but led them toward the barn. Fortunately, the barn doors were partially open, and they slipped inside.

Sara Jane noticed large bales of hay in the loft and a partial one on the floor. There were also three large wooden barrels and some old farm equipment. On the other side was an area designated for garden equipment. She decided to hide behind the barrels, reasoning that they were toward the back and out of the way and large enough to cover her and the wagon.

"Buddy, we're gonna rest quietly here, OK? We've got a little bit of fish left. Would you like some?"

Buddy just whined pitifully and refused the food. She ate most of the piece, then offered the rest to the kind black dog who had led them to the barn. The dog happily gobbled up the fish.

"Little dog, I thank you for your help. You are welcome to stay as long as you want, as long as you don't bark or bring anyone here."

The dog wagged his tail as if understanding.

Sara Jane continued to quietly explore the barn. On the gardening side, she found a wire box filled with potatoes, carrots, and tomatoes. She took only one of each so no one would miss them, then dashed back to her hiding place.

Just as she settled down, she heard footsteps on the gravel path outside the barn. She heard a woman's voice say, "Well, hello, Queenie. What are you up to?"

Sara Jane peeked through a space between the barrels and saw the woman from the garden remove her straw hat and lean down to pet the black dog that Sara Jane now knew was named Queenie. The woman was very pretty with her slender figure and long, wavy, golden hair pulled into a ponytail. She had a warm smile and brown eyes that tugged at Sara Jane's heart as she reminded her of her mother.

Queenie remained with the woman as she sorted the vegetables she had brought into the barn. The woman then removed her straw hat and dirty garden apron and gloves. She selected a few vegetables and left the barn, Queenie following along behind her.

Sara Jane sneaked up to the barn door and peeked through a crack, making sure the woman was going into the house. As the woman opened the screen door, Queenie sat on the porch near the door, not daring to enter the house, and a large multi-colored cat meowed loudly as it climbed out from under one of the rockers.

The woman paused, leaning down to pet the cat, saying, "Hello, Methuselah. Have you been a good boy today?" The cat purred its answer as if saying, "Well, of course. Aren't I always?"

The screened door squeaked shut as the woman continued into the house.

Sara Jane returned to Buddy and tried to get him to drink, but he refused. His head had swollen even more, and she was afraid that he might die. She felt helpless to save him but attempted to tend to his wound. She cleaned off the wound and applied some antiseptic cream, knowing it might not help but feeling like she had to do something. At least Buddy was lying still, which would slow down the speed of the venom through his body.

She racked her brain, thinking back to what her father had taught her about poisonous snake bites, then she had a memory flash of her father putting chopped-up onion covered with wet moss on their neighbor's dog when it had been bitten by a copperhead. Having no other options, she crossed to the gardening side of the barn and searched for an onion. Finding several, she took one over to the barrel, peeled it, then chopped it up with her father's pocket knife. Not having any moss, she wet some of the remaining gauze bandages and, after placing the onions on Buddy's wound, carefully wrapped the gauze bandage around the onions. Her father's reasoning was that the onion would draw out and absorb some of the venom from his body, possibly saving his life.

Queenie came into the barn, sniffed Buddy, then lay down beside him. Sara Jane petted her and thanked her for her support. At the sound of wheels on gravel, Queenie dashed out of the barn. A pickup truck had just pulled up in front of the barn. Sara Jane heard a squeaky truck door open, and a man said, "Thanks, Hank. See you tomorrow!". He attempted to shut the door, but it wouldn't quite close.

"Hank, when are you gonna fix this darn door?"

Another man replied, "Not today, for sure!" Then the door was pulled shut, and the man drove off.

Laughing, the first man opened the barn door, tossed in a tow sack, then walked off.

Sara Jane sneaked to the barn door and peeked through as Queenie joyfully greeted a tall, lanky man with dark hair. He leaned down and rubbed Queenie's head.

"Hey, girl! How ya doing? Did you miss me?"

Queenie wagged her tail and jumped up and down in excitement. The man crossed onto the porch, greeting Methuselah, who meowed half-heartedly, as cats often do, careful not to show too much affection.

As the man opened the screen door, he called out, "Hey, sweetie. What smells so good?"

Sara Jane could smell the food and realized she was hungry. She ate the last apple and the few remaining dewberries, saving the last of the fish for Buddy should he feel like eating. She checked on him and saw he seemed to be asleep. At least for now, he was out of pain.

Sometime later, Sara Jane heard the screen door open, as the couple walked onto the porch, fed Queenie and Methuselah, and sat in their rocking chairs, enjoying the nice spring evening.

"Your flowers sure look nice. What kind are those pink ones?" asked the man.

"Those are petunias. The white flowering shrubs are bridal wreaths, and the taller purple and blue ones are Iris. Of course, you know the rose bushes you gave me to plant. They are my favorites."

"Well, you sure have a green thumb. It's not easy getting things to bloom around here."

"Sam, would it be possible to use the pickup tomorrow? I want to take some chicken soup and a cobbler to Miss Nellie Bell. Ezelle called and told me she fell while gardening."

"No problem. Hank and I will be shoeing the horses tomorrow so we can use his truck. How old is Miss Nellie Bell now?"

"She just turned ninety-four. Ninety-four and still gardening and playing the piano."

"Yes, gardening, playing the piano, and minding other people's business," replied Sam, laughing.

"I have to hand it to her. Despite her age, she keeps her spirits up and continues doing things she loves. Oh, look, Sam, lightning bugs! I have always loved lightning bugs. My sister and I would chase them and try to catch them and put them in a jar with holes in the lid," said Laura, smiling at the memory

"Must be a girl thing," said Sam. "My brother and I just swatted as many mosquitoes as possible".

"Speaking of which," said Laura, "they seem to be out as well."

"Guess we better go in."

As they rose and went inside, Sara Jane was filled with sweet memories of her own parents and the sweet connection between them. How she missed them! She returned to check on Buddy, who was starting to rouse some and give a little whine. Sara Jane pulled up an old milking stool and spoke to Buddy, "Buddy, go back to sleep now, OK? You're gonna be OK."

She gently stroked Buddy's fur and sang to him softly until he fell back asleep.

Exhausted, Sara Jane lay down on the hay to sleep, but she couldn't get her mind to be quiet. Troubling thoughts ran through her head: Would Buddy live through the night? Was Howard still alive and looking for her? Was the sheriff looking for her? Where would they go next? How would they live? Was all this her fault? She tossed and turned, then finally started to fall asleep as she heard in her head, "I am with you always."

CHAPTER 15

BIBLE STORIES

The next morning, Sara awoke to the sound of a rooster crowing. She rose, crossed to the barn door, and saw the lady and her husband standing near the man called Hank's old pickup truck.

"Give Miss Nellie Bell a hug for me," said the man as he hugged his wife.

"I will. I'll be back in time for lunch."

The man climbed in and attempted to close the broken door.

"Hank," said the woman, "Are you ever gonna get that door fixed?"

"I would, Miss Laura," said Hank, "but I'm afraid if I try to fix it, the rest of the truck will fall apart!"

Laughing, he pulled away, spitting tobacco out his window and leaving a trail of dust behind.

The woman then smiled, shook her head, and picked up a basket covered with a red and white checkered cloth. She then crossed to the side of the barn, got in the pickup truck and drove off.

Sarah Jane was amazed to see a woman driving a pickup truck. She greeted Queenie, who ran into the barn, and Methuselah, who was still reserving her judgement as to Sara Jane's character. Sara Jane crossed into the house and into the kitchen. She looked around and found some Mercurochrome. She hated the stuff because it stung when her mother put it on her wounds, but she knew it healed, so she took it, along with some gauze bandages. She found some biscuits left over from breakfast and some fried ham slices and took one of each. She also filled a cup with some milk, then hurried back outside, stopping to give Methuselah a tiny bit of the milk in her bowl.

"Here, Methuselah. This is for not tattlin' on me, OK?

Sara Jane then returned to the barn, where she found Queenie sitting next to Buddy. She looked up as Sara Jane entered. Sara Jane placed the supplies and food on top of one of the barrels.

"How's he doin', Queenie? I brought him some milk." Sara Jane checked Buddy, whose head was swollen even more. Her heart sank. She lifted Buddy's head slightly and managed to get him to drink a small amount of milk.

"That's a good boy, Buddy. You have to get your strength back."

Sara Jane then placed the cup on the barrel and ate half the biscuit and ham, careful to save the rest for the evening. She then realized her own wound from the fish fins was throbbing. She removed the gauze bandage and saw that the wound looked infected. She had been so busy taking care of Buddy that she had neglected herself. She washed off the wound, put Mercurochrome on it, then wrapped it back up. She decided to sneak back into the house and see if there was any aspirin to help the pain and infection.

"O.K., cat, one more time. I'll be right back out."

Sara Jane went back into the kitchen and found a small bottle of aspirin and dashed back out the door and into the barn. She grabbed her canteen and refilled it from the outside water pump, then swallowed one aspirin.

Having not slept much the previous night, Sara Jane lay down to rest. Try as she might, she could not settle down. She remembered how her mother used to tell her stories from the Bible when she couldn't sleep, so Sara Jane told Buddy she would share a story with him.

"You'll like this story, Buddy. It has dogs in it. Once upon a long, long time ago, God became very angry with all the people in the world because they did wicked things and didn't worship Him like they were supposed to. He said, 'I know what I'll do; I will flood the whole world and wash away all the wicked people and start all over.' Then he remembered that there was this man called Noah who wasn't bad like the other folk, so he decided to save Noah and his family. God warned Noah that a great big flood was comin'. He told Noah to build a big 'ol boat called an ark, so Noah got busy building this boat.

Bang, bang, bang! Pound, pound, pound! All Noah's hammerin' and sawin' got on the neighbor's nerves. They thought Noah was crazy. 'What in the world are you buildin', Noah? It ain't rained in months. How are you gonna get that big ol' boat in the water?' But Noah just ignored them and kept on bangin' and poundin'.

Weeks and weeks went by, and finally, the ark was ready. Noah was very smart and had built a large ramp that led up to the boat so the animals could get on. Suddenly, all types of animals started arrivin'. Now, how they knew to come, I don't know. I guess God told them to, and you just don't say "No" to God. Anyway, there were elephants and giraffes and monkeys and dogs and cats and coyotes and armadillos and lots of other animals. They all came two by two.

Now, I'm not sure, but I guess God wanted two of each so He would have a spare in case somethin' happened to one of them.

As soon as Noah loaded up his family, God sealed them in, and it started to rain. It rained and rained and rained for forty days and forty nights until the whole world was covered in water, and all the evil people drowned.

Once the water went away enough, Noah, his family, and all the animals got off and started the world fresh."

"Did you like that story, Buddy?"

Buddy was sound asleep, but Queenie was attentive as though expecting another story.

"I'm glad you liked the story, Queenie. That's all for the night, but I'll tell you another one sometime."

Queenie dutifully lay down by Buddy. Sara Jane realized she was finally sleepy enough and lay down on the hay.

CHAPTER 16

MISS NELLIE BELL

As Laura drove to Rockdale, she smiled as her thoughts turned to Miss Nellie Bell. Laura had just finished reading a new book called **Gone With the Wind.** Her favorite character in the book was an old woman named Aunt Pittypat, who reminded her of Miss Nellie Bell with her old-fashioned corkscrew curls that bounced, her love of talking, and her habit of gossiping.

Laura had known Miss Nellie Bell most of her life, as she was Miss Helen's lifelong best friend. Miss Helen always brought Laura to visit with Miss Nellie Bell whenever Laura's family visited her. Laura always looked forward to these visits. Miss Nellie Bell was devastated when her friend Helen died, so Laura made a point of visiting her, knowing it helped heal her loneliness.

Laura was fascinated with Miss Nellie Bell's house. It was a huge, three-story house that took up a large corner lot. The house boasted several turrets, porches, and decorative trim. The porch on the ground floor wrapped all the way around the house. Laura was told the style was Victorian, but due to its dark color, it looked a little Gothic to her, not unlike a huge, elaborate, chocolate birthday cake. Built in 1899, the house, if not the oldest in Rockdale, was certainly the finest.

The yard had a wooden picket fence that ran the perimeter of the entire lot. A lovely stone pathway led up to the large front steps with flowers planted on either side. Her flower beds were Miss Nellie Bell's pride and joy, and it was because of her love of flower gardening that she had been injured.

As a child, this house fascinated Laura, and she enjoyed exploring all its nooks and crannies. She especially loved the large spiral staircase with the huge chandelier. Laura would pretend to be a princess, slowly making her way from the top of the stairs to the bottom. She wasn't allowed to go any further than the second floor, but that was plenty to keep her busy. Laura's sister refused to come with Laura and Miss Helen to visit Miss Nellie Bell. She finally confessed that she had once seen a woman peering out of a window of a tiny room at the very top of the house and believed it was a ghost that haunted the house. Fine with Laura, she could have the house all to herself.

One day, when Laura was around eight years old, Miss Nellie Bell showed her a secret room behind a bookcase. She told Laura that that is where they hid when pirates invaded their house looking for treasure and rum. Laura's eyes grew wide. Then Miss Nellie Bell laughed until she had tears running down her cheeks at Laura's naivete. When she saw Laura's disappointment and embarrassment, she hugged her and apologized.

"I'm sorry, dear one, I just couldn't help myself. The room was my husband's idea of a safe room should we ever need to hide. We never did, but it was nice knowing it was there."

Laura consoled herself by promising to hide in it and jump out and scare her sister should she ever visit again.

Miss Nellie Bell was a wonderful pianist. She gave piano lessons after her husband died. Laura loved sitting beside her on the bench of the beautiful mahogany piano while Miss Nellie Bell played beautiful songs by Mozart and Beethoven, among others. Whenever Laura visited, she would teach her a little bit, but Laura never visited for more than a few hours each time, so she didn't really have a chance to learn much. She sometimes wished she had a piano of her own and the time to learn how to play.

Laura pulled up to the curb in front of the house, got out, and retrieved the basket of food she had brought. As she walked down the sidewalk to the front steps, she missed not hearing Miss Nellie Bell playing the piano.

"Knock, knock!" called Laura.

A slender, middle-aged black woman answered the door.

"Welcome, Miss Laura. Come on in. Miss Nellie Bell is expecting you."

"Thank you, Ezelle. You're looking good."

"Thank you kindly, Miss Laura. You sure are gonna make Miss Nellie Bell's day."

Ezelle lowered her voice and said, "Miss Laura, you might hafta speak a little louder to her. She won't admit it, but she's startin' to lose her hearin'."

Ezelle led Laura into the parlor, where Miss Nellie Bell was reclining on a chaise lounge in all her glory. Laura never remembers seeing her when she wasn't dressed beautifully, perfect corkscrew curls bouncing, and a little too much make-up.

"Laura! Come here, my dear, and give me a great big ol' hug!" said Miss Nellie Bell.

Laura crossed to her and hugged her, noticing some bruising on her face and arm. Her ankle was in a cast.

"Miss Nellie Bell, what have you done to yourself? You keep on gardening, and next time, you'll break a hip or worse."

Miss Nellie Bell laughed her unique tinkling laugh and said, "I know. I know. I've already been lectured by Ezelle, Odell, the doctor, the preacher, and my neighbors. But you know how much I love working in my flower beds."

"I do, but we worry about you. We want you to be around a lot longer."

Miss Nellie Belle laughed again and said, "Why, Laura, dear. I'm ninety-four years old. Just how long do you expect me to live? And how is that sweet husband of yours?"

"Sam is good. He says to give you a hug."

"One of these days, he needs to give me a hug in person. Ezelle, will you please bring Miss Laura a chair she can put next to me?"

"Yes'um."

"Now, what do you have in that basket? Oh my, I sound like the Big Bad Wolf!" said Miss Nellie Bell, laughing.

Laura laughed as she set the basket at the foot of the chaise lounge.

"I made chicken soup and a dewberry cobbler."

"Oh, my favorite cobbler! Thank you, dear. I'll have both for lunch. Ezelle, will you please place Laura's basket in the kitchen?"

"Yes'um," said Ezelle, placing the chair near the chaise lounge.

As Ezelle left, Laura asked, "How long have Ezelle and Odell been with you?"

"Let me see, " said Miss Nellie Bell, "Joseph hired them before he died, and that was thirty years ago, so thirty-one years, I guess. I don't know what I would do without them."

Laura agreed. She knew that Ezelle kept the house and did the cooking, as well as providing companionship for Miss Nellie Bell. Her husband Odell kept the grounds, did repairs, and ran errands. They lived in the guest cottage on the property.

Ezelle returned with a glass of iced tea for them both and set it on a tray table next to the chaise lounge.

"Thank you, Ezelle," said Laura. Laura noticed some framed photos on the piano she had not seen before. She rose to look at them more closely. She lifted the first one and Miss Nellie Belle said, "That's my Joseph and I on our wedding day. I was wearing my mother's wedding dress. The couple with us are your Great- Aunt Helen and her fiancé Luke. Sadly, Luke was killed at Antietam just a few months after this picture was taken. He had volunteered with the Texan Brigade that fought for the confederacy. Your poor aunt was despondent."

"How awful! I had no idea."

"She never spoke of it, nor did I. It was just too painful. She never loved anyone else and refused to marry."

"And who is this?" asked Laura, holding up a framed photo of a little girl around five or six years old.

Miss Nellie Bell's eyes filled with tears as she said, "That's my sweet Sally. My only child. She died from scarlet fever when she was only six. What a blessing she was while we had her!"

"I'm so very sorry, Miss Nellie Bell. I didn't mean to bring up sad memories."

"That is something that you and I share, Laura. The grief over losing one's only child. There is no pain as awful. It never goes away, Laura, but I promise you that it will get better. God helps us endure all things."

Laura fought back her tears.

"But we have been blessed in so many other ways, haven't we, Laura? I had the dearest husband in the world for almost fifty years, and you have your wonderful Sam."

Changing the topic, Miss Nellie Bell said, "Have you heard about that terrible fire a few days ago?"

"Only that the entire house burned to the ground. I didn't know the people who lived there, did you?"

"Yes, dear, I did, indeed. They found the completely burned body of a man in the house and are assuming it is the body of Howard Mills, who lived there. His precious stepdaughter, Sara Jane, lived with him, but no one has located her. Last I heard, the authorities were waiting until the fire rubble completely cooled off to do further digging in the house."

"Oh, I do hope she is found alive and unharmed," said Laura.

"Yes, indeed. I met her, you know, she and her lovely mother and father, before they both died. That was a few years back when the child couldn't have been more than five or six. I had gone into town to pick up some supplies. Odell usually did this, but the poor dear had the flu. Anyway, a lovely couple and a little girl approached me and offered to load everything for me. I happily agreed. They followed me home and unloaded everything and took the supplies into the house. I had such a lovely feeling about these three that I invited them in for tea.

They introduced themselves as James and Mary Evans, and their little girl was Sara Jane. Oh, they were delightful! The little girl was fascinated by the piano, so I lifted her onto the bench and sat beside her. I played some Brahms and Mozart. She seemed mesmerized. I showed her middle C on the keyboard and a few other notes. She seemed to have a natural gift, so I told her parents I would love to give her lessons for free. They were delighted and promised to come by next time they were in town.

Unfortunately, that was never to be. A few weeks later, James was killed in a farming equipment accident. The mother and child were left to manage the small farm by themselves, and I never saw them again."

"How awful!" said Laura. "What happened to the mother?"

"What happened was that she met and married Howard Mills several months later, and he changed their lives for the worse. Howard was a good-looking young man who was a real charmer with the ladies. He ran the general store here in Rockdale. He was pleasant enough and hadn't been involved in any scandals that I knew of. Rumors were that he liked to drink a little too much sometimes, but that was true of most men in this town.

Anyway, they seemed happy for a while until the economy got worse, and he almost lost the farm. The store was suffering, as well. Rumor has it he started drinking more, which is never good. Then, a year later, Mary died after giving birth to a premature baby who only lived a couple of hours. She died shortly after."

"That poor family endured so much tragedy! Especially the little girl," said Laura.

"Yes, indeed," said Miss Nellie Bell. "And it was not over yet. The death of his wife and baby caused Howard to go into a deep depression filled with anger, which some say he took out on the little girl. No one has seen her in months because he stopped going to church and took her out of school, saying he needed her to run the household."

"And then the tragic fire. I sure hope the little girl is OK and has a chance of a better life." She paused as she took another sip of tea." They must have quit attending church right before Sam and I moved here and joined the church," said Laura.

"'Scuse me, Miss Laura, but it's time for Miss Nellie Bell's pill and lunch," said Ezelle.

"Yes, please join me, Laura."

"Thank you so much, "said Laura, "but I need to get going. I promised Sam I would be home by lunchtime."

"Well, come hug me good-bye. And thanks so much for the soup and cobbler. Give Sam a hug and drive carefully."

Ezelle walked Laura to the door, and Laura said, "Ezelle, you have my phone number. Don't hesitate to call me if she needs anything, OK?"

"Yes'um, Miss Laura. Thank you so much for coming."

Laura climbed into the truck and drove home, the conversation with Miss Nellie Bell still troubling her mind.

CHAPTER 17

O BROTHER MAN

Sheriff Grady Black sat in his desk chair, his long legs sporting cowboy boots that rested on top of his desk at his office in Cameron. His Stetson hat was tilted to shade his eyes, and anyone looking in might think he was napping, except for the twine he kept wrapping and unwrapping around his left hand.

This was the sheriff's thinking position, where he worked out dilemmas and answers to problems. The fire and death of Howard Mills bothered him. On the one hand, it was simple: the house somehow caught fire, and Mills, a known heavy drinker, had passed out from alcohol and was unable to save himself.

But what if the fire was deliberate? What if someone wanted to kill Howard Mills? Did he have any enemies? What was to be gained by his death? And what about the child? Her body was not found. Had she been in the house when the fire started but managed to escape? If so, where was she? Why hadn't she sought help? Had she been visiting family the day of the fire? As far as the sheriff knew, there was no family.

Nellie Bell Richards, one of Rockdale's oldest and most influential citizens, as well as his grandmother's cousin, had called him to express her concern over the child, and this renewed his interest in the case.

With the help of volunteers from the community and the Sandy Creek Methodist Church the child's family had once attended, they had searched an area up to half a mile in each direction, concentrating on the road and the woods. They obviously needed to expand their search.

Sheriff Black sat up and called out to his deputy, "Mark, come here a minute, will ya?"

The deputy Mark Hughes dutifully appeared. "Whatcha need, sheriff?"

"I need you to get hold of all those volunteers from the search and try to add some more. Get some from all the other churches in Rockdale. That kid must be out there somewhere, and if she is, we need to find her. She could be badly injured and in danger. We're gonna set up a grid two miles wide in every direction and assign people to each one."

"Sure thing, sheriff."

"Maybe then Nellie Bell Richards will get off my back!"

The deputy smiled as he left to contact the Baptist, Lutheran, Methodist, Presbyterian, and Catholic church leaders. He knew that there was a certain urgency to the search, not just for the safety of the little girl but also for appearances. This was an election year, and Sheriff Grady just found out that William Conrad, the publisher and editor of the Rockdale weekly newspaper, **The Rockdale Reporter and Messenger**, was seriously considering running against him for sheriff. Sheriff Black had been sheriff of Milam County for twelve years. The only time anyone dared run against him was when his former deputy, Charles Thrasher, got the big head and decided he wanted to be sheriff.

That had been a big mistake, as Sheriff Black won the election in a landslide vote. The joke around town was that the only folks who voted for Charles were his mother, himself, and his latest girlfriend, who dumped him shortly afterwards. His mother consoled him by saying, "It's not that no one likes you, Charles. It's just that they like Sheriff Black more. Now lick your wounds, hold your head up, and ask for your job back." But being too proud and stubborn, Charles sacked groceries for almost a year before being hired on in Rockdale. This was when Mark had been hired.

But this new challenger was different. Mr. Conrad was well-liked and respected and could be a worthy opponent. Plus, he had the power of the press. Mark could just imagine headlines like "Helpless Girl Still Not Found" or an editorial about whether the sheriff was doing enough to find her. Well, we will just have to wait and see. Personally, Mark liked Grady Black and hoped he would win.

CHAPTER 18

WE'VE A STORY TO TELL

Sara Jane was awakened by the sound of the motor and wheels on the gravel as Laura arrived home. She peeked out the barn door as Laura parked the truck and walked into the house carrying the basket and red and white checkered cloth.

As Laura approached the porch, Queenie ran to greet her, happily wagging her tail. Laura bent down to rub her head. "Hello, my sweet little dog." Noticing that Methuselah was not in her usual place on the porch, Laura called out, "Kitty! Methuselah! Where are you?"

Laura crossed into the house, where Methuselah sat on the back of a chair facing the window. "Meow!" cried the cat.

"There you are! What on earth are you doing in the house?" Laura carried Methuselah to the porch and sat her in a rocker, then headed back in just as Sam and Hank arrived.

"How on earth did Methuselah get in the house?" asked Sam.

"I have no idea. I distinctly remember seeing her under one of the rockers when I was leaving."

"Well, you could be wrong. You did just turn twenty-five, and old people get confused sometimes," said Sam, sporting a big grin and a twinkle in his eye.

"Very funny," said Laua. "Ya'll come on in, and I'll make you a sandwich."

Sara Jane realized that Methuselah probably slipped in when she had gone back in the house for the aspirin. She vowed to be more careful. She checked on Buddy, who, thankfully, did not feel as hot and was breathing normally.

Queenie came back into the barn, tail wagging.

"Good news, Queenie," said Sara Jane, "Buddy seems to be doing better."

As if in response to the good news, Queenie crossed to Buddy, stood up on her hind legs, and, holding on to the side of the wagon, licked Buddy's head.

Sara Jane heard the screen door open. Once again, she peeked through an opening in the barn doors and saw Laura, Sam, and Hank cross onto the front porch.

Hank, Sam, and Laura each held a plate with a sandwich and a glass of what looked like iced tea. They all sat and began eating.

"So, how was Miss Nellie Bell?" asked Sam.

"Pretty good, considering she had a bad fall. She's in good spirits, as usual, and sends you a hug but wants you to give her one in person."

Sam laughed and took another bite of the sandwich.

"Did y'all get the horses shoed?" asked Laura.

"Almost done. Got three more to go," said Hank. "Miss Laura, you make the best sweet tea I ever had."

"Why, thank you, Hank."

Sam rose, wiping his hands on his jeans and giving his wife a peck on the cheek. "Guess we better get going, Hank. Those horses won't shoe themselves."

"Yessir. Miss Laura, I thank you kindly for the lunch."

"You are most welcome, Hank."

They got in the pickup truck, the old door squeaking and difficult to close as usual. "I know, I know," laughed Hank as they drove off, leaving a trail of dust.

"We sure do need rain," said Laura to herself. She stacked up the dishes and went back into the house.

Sara Jane sat on the milking stool next to Buddy and stroked his head. "Buddy, they keep talkin' about Miss Nellie Bell in Rockdale. I'm thinkin' that's the nice old lady who was gonna teach me piano. It was a long time ago, but it must be her. How many people have a name like that? Wouldn't it be somethin' if that was her?"

That evening after supper, Sam and Laura sat in the porch rockers, sipping on their lemonade.

"I didn't want to give away too much about my visit to Miss Nellie Bell while Hank was here," said Laura. "But I learned a lot I never knew."

"Like what?" asked Sam.

"Did you know her only child died from scarlet fever?"

"No. That's awful."

Laura then told Sam about Miss Helen and the death of her fiancé'.

"That is so tragic," said Sam, "I had no idea."

"Sam, did you hear about that fire a few miles from us?"

"Yes. Entire house burned down. I didn't know the folks who lived there."

"Well, it turns out Miss Nellie Bell knew the family. She said a man's burned body was found in the house. They assume it was Howard Mills who lived there. They are worried about the little girl, his stepdaughter, who lived with him. Nobody knows where she is or if she's OK."

"Guess we'll have to keep a lookout," said Sam.

"That poor child has been through so much. Both her parents died, her stepfather was an alcoholic and may have abused her, and now this fire," added Laura.

"That poor kid! Nobody should have to endure all that. Life sure isn't fair sometimes."

Laura and Sam went back into the house when the first mosquitoes started biting.

Sara Jane had been listening, and her heart started to pound. Howard was dead! She didn't have to worry about him anymore! Relieve flooded her body, quickly followed by guilt at being glad he was dead. She hoped the terrible nightmares would now end. She still feared that the sheriff might think she killed him or that she and Buddy would be discovered. She vowed to leave the farm as soon as Buddy was well enough to travel.

Queenie entered the barn, crossed to Buddy, and looked up expectantly. "Oh, I see. You want another Bible story? OK. Here's one of my favorites. It's about a shepherd boy named David and a giant named Goliath. Now, the Israeli folks were at war with a ferocious group of people called the Filly Stines, and as each group gathered on one side or the other of a valley, things were not looking good for the Israeli folk. Not only were these Filly Stines known to be fierce warriors, but they also wore lots of armor, had weapons, and were really big. Plus, there were lots and lots of them.

Anyway, the biggest one of them, Goliath, came stomping out from the others. Stomp, stomp, stomp! went his big 'ol steps. Then he yelled, 'Hey, you people! Send out your best man and let him fight me, and whoever wins our fight will be declared the winner of this battle.'

But the Israeli folk weren't real anxious to send anyone out, so Goliath yelled, 'What, are you chicken? Surely you have one person big and brave enough to fight me.'

Still, none of the Israeli folk answered him.

Now, David, a shepherd boy, was very close to God. He told the other Israeli folk that he would fight Goliath, but they thought that was pretty dumb. 'You have no weapons or armor. How do you think you can kill this giant man?'

David said, 'God has told me he will be with me, so I am not afraid. I will use my slingshot and five smooth stones, and I will kill him like I kill the wolves who try to hurt my sheep.'

Well, the Israeli folk said, 'What the heck, we don't have anyone else volunteerin', so go ahead, David.'

So, David faced Goliath, who laughed and said, 'Are you kiddin' me? Is this the best you've got?' Then he got mad and said, 'You dare to insult me with this shepherd boy! Well, I will kill him quickly!'

Goliath pulled his giant sword, and before he could take a step, David hit him in the forehead with a rock from his slingshot! Zing! Goliath fell on his face, and the fall shook the earth. Then David cut off Goliath's big 'ol head and carried it around to show the Israeli folk, who cheered and cheered!"

"Did y'all like that story?" Queenie wagged her tail, and Buddy gave a tiny bark, so Sara Jane took that as a "yes'.

When Laura and Sam were getting into bed that night, Laura said, "Sam, I hesitate to say anything because I don't want to worry you unnecessarily, but I think someone has been coming into the house."

"Coming into the house? What makes you think so?" asked Sam.

"Remember when Methuselah got into the house? I am positive she was on the porch when I left. Also, I thought it was my imagination, but for the last two days, some food has gone missing. Not a lot, but some biscuits, cheese, hard-boiled eggs, things like that."

"It's probably another hobo on his way to the railroad in Rockdale. More and more people are losing their homes and jobs. We can't stop them from coming by, and I'd like to help them, but I don't like the idea of them coming into the house, especially when you are here alone. Let's try this: leave a small sack of food on the porch and write 'Free Food' on it. Put Queenie and Methuselah in the house to keep them from getting the food, and close and lock the door when you leave to work in the garden or the chicken coop."

"That's a good idea. Hopefully, the person will get the hint that we are on to him and be on his way."

"If he stays longer, I'll search the farm and make sure he leaves." said Sam.

CHAPTER 19

THE SEARCH BEGINS

It was just after sunrise the next day when the volunteers started gathering at the Sandy Creek Methodist Church. Mark had done a great job of enlisting the help of the community. More than a hundred people stood ready to help.

Sheriff Black stood on the top step of the church steps and said, "Thank you all for coming out. Ya'll know who we're lookin' for. This child could be hurt or in danger, so it is important that we find her. Deputy Mark Hughes is gonna pass out a grid map to each group in a coupla minutes, but before we get started, I'd like to hear from any of you who knew her and might know something about this child."

A red-haired lady raised her hand. "She and her family used to come here every Sunday, but we haven't seen her since her mamma died."

"Yes'm," replied the sheriff, "anything else?"

Another woman raised her hand and spoke, "She was in the same grade as my Amy and was real smart. Amy said she ain't seen her or her dog in school for months, somethin' about her stepdaddy taking her out of school to keep the house and help with the farm."

There was some grumbling from the crowd. A man raised his hand and spoke, "Now, let's not be too quick to criticize the man. We don't know the whole story."

Another woman raised her hand and spoke, "Well, I, for one, feel guilty about not checking on that child. She was a member of our church family."

"Now Margaret," said Pastor Chris, the Methodist minister, "don't beat yourself up over that. I and two of our deacons went to their house in the weeks following her mother's death, and Howard Mills made it clear he wanted us off his property. You can't help someone who doesn't want to be helped."

"Maybe we should have asked the sheriff to check on the girl?" said a man in the crowd.

"For what reason?" responded another volunteer.

"Look, folks," said Sheriff Black, "this isn't gettin' us anywhere. What can you tell me that might help us find her? What does she look like? Not all of us know."

"Well," said the red- headed lady, "she's nine years old, but tall for her age, like her Daddy. She has brown hair and eyes and likes to wear her hair in pigtails."

"Good," said the sheriff. "That's helpful. Now somebody mentioned a dog?"

"Yes," said another church member. "She has a dog named Buddy that goes everywhere with her. He is a brown and white scruffy-lookin' mutt. He even used to lie on the church porch while she was inside. Wherever she is, that dog will be with her."

"Great," said the sheriff. "That's very helpful. OK, everybody, please get in groups of 6-8 and choose a group leader. Deputy

Hughes will give each group leader a copy of the grid map and tell you which area you'll be searching. He will also give you a whistle. If any person sees something, just blow your whistle, and the other team members will come to you. Let's meet back here at 11:00. The kind ladies of Sandy Creek Methodist have offered to make lunch for us. Any questions? Ok, good luck, everybody."

CHAPTER 20

FREE FOOD

The next morning, Sara Jane awoke later than usual. Her exhaustion had finally caught up with her. She had slept through the rooster crowing and Sam and Hank leaving to go to the field. She peeked out the barn doors and saw that the house door was closed. "That's odd," said Sara. She looked around to make sure no one was in sight and dashed to the front porch. She tried the door, which was locked, and realized she did not see Queenie or Methuselah on the porch.

Puzzled, she saw the sack of "Free Food" in one of the rockers. She dashed back to the barn, opened the sack, and saw that along with the food was a note that said, "Hello, my brother. We have noticed you have come into our house for food. We want to help you, but we ask that you not enter our house again. We will leave you one more sack of food tomorrow. Then we ask that you be on your way."

Sara Jane started to shake. They knew she was here! Or did they? The note said "brother". Sara Jane realized she had to leave tomorrow at the latest. She hoped and prayed that Buddy would be well enough to travel. All she could do now is pray and wait.

CHAPTER 21

STILL MISSING

The volunteers began trickling back to the Sandy Creek Methodist Church at 11:00 AM. Only one whistle had been blown, and that was when one of the team members came across a child's shoe, which they later determined was for a much smaller child. Disappointed, they all sat down to eat the nice meal the church ladies had prepared for them.

No one was more disappointed than Sheriff Black, who was, quite honestly, running out of ideas. Where could that child be? He dreaded reporting to Miss Nellie Bell and envisioned the negative newspaper headline., "Sheriff Fails to Find Lost Child."

After everyone had eaten, the sheriff thanked them all and asked that they all remain vigilante. As he and Deputy Hughes walked to the car, he said, "Mark, does your brother still have those bloodhounds?"

"Sure does. Why? Think we should use 'em?"

"Yep. This time, we'll concentrate around the Evans/Mills property. I hate to even say it, but there's a chance Mills may have killed the girl and buried her somewhere on the property."

"Let's hope not," said the deputy, "but I'll call my brother and get the dogs lined up."

"Great. We also need to find something that belonged to the child. Maybe the dogs can follow the scent."

Sheriff Black was not hopeful they would find anything. After all, the entir house had burned down. But he had to try.

CHAPTER 22

PRECIOUS OBJECTS

Sara Jane sat down by Buddy, who seemed to be more alert but still weak. She was able to get him to eat a little of the hard-boiled egg and drink some water, a good sign. Sara Jane realized she missed Queenie and knew Buddy did as well. She felt guilty that it was because of her that Queenie and Methuselah were locked in the house.

Sara Jane sang to Buddy as she gently stroked his fur. Her thoughts turned to her mother and how she sang to her at bedtime. Her eyes filled with tears, and she suddenly felt panicked. She had to hold something that belonged to her mother to calm her. She grabbed her rucksack and pawed through it like a drowning person in search of a life-preserver. She pulled out her mother's tin sewing box and held it to her chest, eyes closed and heart pounding.

"Oh, Mama, sometimes I miss you so much I feel like my heart is just gonna break!" Tears rolled down her cheeks as she opened the box and pulled out one-by-one the precious objects within. The first object was her mother's thimble, which she put on her finger. Her family didn't have much, but they never made Sara Jane feel poor. Somehow, her mother made sure Sara Jane had clothes to wear. The last thing her mother had made her was her Easter dress made from a flour sack. It was a floral print, and her mother had added a collar made from one of Sara Jane's old dresses. Her mother explained that the people who made the sacks for flour realized that people were using their sacks to make clothing, so they started making their sacks in floral prints instead of the plain white ones. Sara treasured that dress but had long outgrown it. She kept it in the tree house with other treasured objects.

The next precious object was her mother's silver cross necklace. Her mother had worn this every day. Sara Jane treasured it but was afraid to wear it in case she lost it. She had also been mad at God when her mother died and had not felt worthy to wear it. As she held the cross in her hand, a feeling of love and peace came over her, and she knew her mother wanted her to wear it. She slipped the necklace over her head and immediately felt a stronger connection with her mother.

The next item was the seashell her father had brought her from Galveston. As she held it, she closed her eyes and imagined how wonderful it would be to be at the beach with her parents and Buddy. She could smell the sea air and feel the sand between her toes as they dashed into the ocean, waves crashing around them. She could hear their laughter and the sound of the sea gulls circling above them. She had never been to the beach, but her father had described it so vividly that she felt she was there with him. He had promised to take her but was killed before he could fulfill his promise. Someday, thought Sara Jane, someday.

Sara Jane heard the barn door open and peeked through a crack between the barrels. Laura removed her garden gloves and apron and hung up her straw hat. From a small cart, she removed tomatoes, potatoes, onions, carrots, okra, and purple hull peas. She then chose a couple of tomatoes and an onion and crossed to the front porch and unlocked the door, letting out Queenie and a cranky Methuselah.

Queenie ran into the barn and laid down by Buddy, who had climbed out of the wagon and was sitting up on the hay. They both wagged their tails and licked one another. Sara Jane then heard a loud

"Meow" and looked up to see Methuselah sitting on the top of one of the barrels. She had come to join the party.

That night, Laura and Sam sat on the front porch, telling each other about their day.

"They took the sack of food I left, and I did like you suggested and locked the door with Queenie and Methuselah inside."

"Good. Hopefully, they'll leave tomorrow. They probably wouldn't stay too long in one place for fear of being caught or turned over to the sheriff. The train in Rockdale is only a couple of miles south. They will probably head that way."

"I'll put a little extra food in tomorrow's sack."

Sara Jane had been listening as usual and was grateful for the information. The train! Why hadn't she thought of the train? They could ride the freight train like she heard the hobos did. There was a train depot in Rockdale where she and Buddy could sneak onto a boxcar and ride as far away as they wanted. They might even find a train that traveled to the beach!

That night, Sara Jane lay down and made plans for tomorrow. She thanked God for presenting a way when there didn't seem to be one. The night was quieter than usual. Was that a train whistle she heard off in the distance, or was it only her imagination anticipating their trip?

CHAPTER 23

THE TREE HOUSE

Early the next morning, Sheriff Black met Deputy Hughes and his brother Jeff at the site of the burned-down house. Jeff had two large blood hounds, Woody and Guthrie, on long leashes. They were already circling around, eagerly sniffing the ground.

"Were any livestock injured?" asked the sheriff.

"Didn't have any. Sold off their livestock a year ago."

A pickup they didn't recognize pulled up, and Hal, a member of the Sandy Creek Methodist Church, hopped out. "Mornin' sheriff, I was hopin' I'd run into you."

"Mornin," said the sheriff, "Ya need somethin'?"

"No, but I got some information that might help. My daughter Amy told my wife we should check the treehouse down by the pond. Seems she and Sara Jane had an occasional tea party there back before her mother died. Might be worth a look."

"Much obliged, Hal. We'll take a look."

Hal jumped back in the pickup and drove off.

"Let's check that treehouse and see if there's anything there that has the girl's scent on it."

The men and dogs headed out to search the treehouse. When they found it, Deputy Hughes, the smaller of the two men, volunteered to climb up and check it out. "We're in luck, fellas!" called the deputy from the treehouse, "there's a jar of peaches and an old flour sack dress."

"Great," said the sheriff. "Leave the peaches and bring the dress."

The deputy climbed down and handed the dress to the sheriff, who looked it over, hoping there was no blood on it. He then handed it to Jeff for his dogs to smell.

The dogs got the scent and immediately started barking and sniffing around the grounds around the treehouse. To their surprise, rather than heading back to the burn site, the dogs led them away from the treehouse in the opposite direction.

"Mark," said Jeff, "take Woody here and follow his lead. I'll take Guthrie and do the same."

CHAPTER 24

STEAL AWAY

The next morning, Sara Jane arose to the sound of a rooster crowing. Buddy barked at the sound, surprising her. Although glad he had the strength to bark, Sara Jane feared someone would hear him. "Hush, Buddy! We gotta be quiet."he packed up the rucksack and got ready to leave.

Late last night, after Sam and Laura were asleep, Sara Jane left a bowl of shelled purple hull peas, four nickels, and a note on the porch:

Dear Lady,

Thank you for the food. I shelled these peas for you and am leaving you the rest of my money to help pay for the food. I will leave in the morning as soon as I get your last sack of food. I hope I didn't worry you too much. Goodbye and thanks.

A hobo

After Laura locked the door and headed for the garden, she dashed to the porch, grabbed the sack and dashed back to the barn. She opened the sack, and in addition to extra food, there were four nickels wrapped in a note that said:

Dear Sir,

You are welcome. I am returning your money because you need it more than I do. Good luck, and may God bless you.

Laura

The note caused Sara Jane to tear up. How kind this lady was! Sara Jane put the rucksack on her back and helped Buddy into the wagon, admonishing him to stay in it. Then she grabbed her walking stick and peeked out the barn doors, making sure Laura was nowhere in sight.

As they headed down the road, Buddy started to whine. "I know," said Sara Jane, "I'm sorry we couldn't say good-bye to Queenie and Methuselah, but it's probably for the best. Queenie would want to follow us.

Sara Jane knew that if she followed the road south, she would eventually reach the railroad tracks. She was nervous about being seen, so she planned to walk much of the way closer to the tree line. If all went well, she would reach Rockdale in a couple of hours.

CHAPTER 25

WHERE ARE YOU?

The dogs led the men for over an hour to a spot on the bank of the river. They circled around and barked, then seemed to lose the scent as they approached the water.

"She must have gone into the water, "said Deputy Hughes.

"That don't sound too good," said Sheriff Black. "She could have waded in and drowned, or someone could have thrown her in. Jeff, how much longer can the dogs hunt?"

"I really need to be headin' back," said Jeff, "they can only do this for a few hours a day because it wears them out. Plus, they lose interest after a while if they haven't found anything."

"OK, let's head back to the burn site and load up. Tomorrow, we'll load up the dogs and drive to the spot where we left off today. There's the possibility she may be dead, and we will find her body downstream, or maybe the dogs will pick up her scent again. At least we have a starting point."

This did not look good. Finding a body instead of a live child was everyone's worst nightmare. The only positive thing the sheriff could think of was that if they did find her body, they would have no family to notify.

CHAPTER 26

RAINBOW COURTS

As hoped, Sara Jane and Buddy made it to the railroad tracks without incident. They stopped a couple of times to rest in the shade trees and were a bit slower than usual because Buddy kept getting out of the wagon so he could walk. About half-way there, he gave up and let Sara Jane put him back in the wagon.

"Buddy, I'm not sure which direction to go now. Let's go right, and if we don't reach Rockdale soon, we'll know we went the wrong way."

Fortunately, they only had to walk half a mile before seeing a small sign that said, "Rockdale 1 mile"

"We're in luck, Buddy, only a mile to go!"

As they reached the city limits, Sara Jane realized she was exhausted and needed to rest. She spotted a sign that said "Rainbow Courts" and decided to look around. It was obviously some kind of place where travelers could stay overnight in small cottages. The grounds were nicely manicured, and there were lots of trees at the back of the property. She pulled the wagon toward a copse of trees that would provide shade and protection from being seen.

After eating food from the sack and drinking from the canteen, Sara Jane soon fell asleep, exhausted.

When she awoke, the sun was setting, and rather than try to find the depot in the dark, Sara Jane decided to settle in for the night. It was a pleasant evening. The slight breeze kept away the mosquitoes. Sara Jane looked up at the clear sky that had begun turning an inky blue.

"Look, Buddy, there's the first star! Close your eyes and make a wish with me:

Star light, star bright, first star I see tonight. I wish I may, I wish I might, have the wish I wish tonight.

I bet you wished for the same thing I did, Buddy…a nice home and a family who will love us and be good to us. We had that once, a long time ago, didn't we?" Sara Jane's eyes filled with tears. "Maybe one day we'll have that again, Buddy. Let's not give up hope, OK?"

Now all the stars were out in the clear sky. "Look, Buddy! The stars look like a sky full of lightning bugs. That's a good sign." Sara Jane stroked Buddy's fur as she sang him a lullaby. "Buddy, you are the best dog ever. Tomorrow, we're gonna start a new adventure, and I'm so happy I have you with me."

The sound of the night critters soon lulled her to sleep.

CHAPTER 27

MR. MATTHEW

Sara Jane was awoken by the sound of Buddy barking at a cat that had wandered over to check them out. "Buddy, hush! Leave that cat alone!"

"It's alright, little lady. That ol' cat knows how to take care of himself. He's lived out here a long time."

Startled, Sara Jane noticed an older man wearing crumpled work clothes. He had a beard, and his hair was long, unkept, and, like his beard, starting to gray. He was missing a couple of fingers from his left hand, and he walked with a limp. He was wearing a tool belt and carrying a hammer. She felt an adrenaline rush, and her heart started to pound.

"Sorry if I startled you," said the man.

"That's OK." Although Sara Jane knew to be vigilant around strangers, there was something about this man's presence that calmed her.

"Your folks stayin' here?" asked the man.

"No, sir. My dog and I are just stayin' here for a while, then we're gonna catch the train. Can you tell me how to get to the train depot?"

"Sure can. Which train you takin'?"

"It don't really matter," said Sara Jane, "whichever one leaves next."

"I see. You gonna hop a freight?"

"Yessir. Me and my dog."

"What about your folks? Won't they worry about you?"

"No, sir. My folks are dead."

"Oh, " said the man, "I'm real sorry. I'll tell you what. If you can hang out here for a couple of hours, I'll go with you to the train. I just got a couple more chores to do, then I'm headin' out."

"Oh, thank you, mister. "

Sara Jane watched as the man walked into one of the cottages and started hammering. She and Buddy shared a biscuit and some beef jerky for breakfast. Sara Jane knew it was risky trusting this stranger, but something about his voice and his kind eyes told her he was harmless. Besides, if he tried to harm her in any way, Buddy would come to her defense.

A couple of hours later, Sara Jane saw the man knock on the office door. A woman Sara Jane assumed was the owner or manager opened the door and greeted him.

The man handed her the hammer and tool belt and said, "I fixed those shelves in #7 and the broken steps in #3."

"That's great, Matthew, thank you so much. Are you sure you can't stay a few more days?"

"No, ma'am. You know I don't like to stay in one place too long. It's time to hit the road."

"Well, you know you are always welcome here, Matthew. We've always got something needin' fixin', and you do great work. The woman handed him an envelope and a small sack. "I made you a sandwich for the road. Safe travels, Matthew. Come back soon."

"Thank you, ma'am," said the man. Then he walked toward Sara Jane, a bedroll on his back and the sack and envelope in his hand.

"OK, little lady," said the man, "you sure you wanna do this?"

"Yessir. Can my dog come, too? I won't go if he can't come, too."

"No problem. Glad to have him with us. I like dogs. Name's Matthew, and who are you?"

"Well, Mr. Matthew, if it's OK with you, I'd rather not tell you right now. Maybe later."

Matthew smiled, and they started walking, "Not a problem. Didn't mean to pry. The depot is about half a mile this way. I gotta pal who works there this time of day. I pay him a dollar, and he lets me sneak on the boxcar, as long as his boss isn't around. We should get there about an hour before the train pulls out. Are you sure it don't matter where the train is goin'?"

"No, sir. I just need to get far away from here. If it's OK with you, I'll take whatever train you're taking."

They continued walking, Matthew wondering what or who this child was running from and how long she had been homeless.

"Matthew!" called a man from the depot, "You're just in time."

"Hey, Fred! I hope it's OK; I've got some company ridin' along."

"Well, I don't like it much. I gotta collect an extra dollar for the girl and fifty cents for the dog."

Matthew handed him three one-dollar bills. "Don't have any change, Fred."

"Me, neither. I'll hang on to the extra fifty cents and credit it to you. And Matthew, don't bring anyone else with you next time. I'm takin' a chance as it is. Go ahead and get on."

"See ya, Fred," said Matthew, helping Sara Jane and Buddy into the boxcar along with the wagon.

He assigned Sara Jane and Buddy one corner, and he took another, careful not to make her feel uncomfortable. "Fred's gotta close the door now, and it might get a little stuffy, but the train'll pull out in about 20 minutes or so."

"Thank you, Mr. Matthew."

As predicted, the train pulled out and headed down the tracks.

"You ride the freight trains a lot, Mr. Matthew?"

"Quite a bit," said Matthew.

Sara Jane hoped it wouldn't make her or Buddy queasy.

She decided she liked the rhythmic clacking of the wheels on the train tracks as they headed out to parts unknown.

CHAPTER 28

CURIOUS

When Laura returned from the garden, she unloaded vegetables into the wire baskets in the barn and removed her apron, gloves, and hat. She leaned the hoe and rack against the barn wall, then crossed to the front porch and let Queenie and Methuselah outside.

She noticed Queenie run to the barn then come back out looking confused and distressed. Queenie then began sniffing the ground, following a scent that led away from the barn. She followed the scent all the way to the road, then stopped, sat, and stared at the road that led away from the farm.

Curious, Laura walked toward Queenie and noticed some type of small wagon wheels and one set of footprints. She called Queenie to follow her into the barn and noticed that Queenie immediately ran to an area behind some barrels. Queenie made a whining sound that Laura thought she was incapable of making. She noticed that the hay was mashed down there and that the wagon wheels and footprints began there.

Whoever had been staying there had obviously been kind to Queenie, who seemed sad that they were gone. Curious.

CHAPTER 29

RIDING THE RAILS

"You have any idea where this train is goin', Mr. Matthew?" asked Sara Jane.

"Yep. We're headin' to Hearne, east of Rockdale. The train usually sits there overnight, then adds some empty boxcars and heads up to Palestine."

"OK, thank you, Mr. Matthew. I was kinda hopin' we might be headed to the beach at Galveston."

"Like the beach, do you? Well, there are trains that go to Galveston, but this ain't one of 'em." Matthew paused, then asked, "Is your dog OK? He hasn't moved much."

"He's still healin' from a rattlesnake bite a few days ago. We was pickin' dewberries, and he got bit on the side of the face. I was afraid he might die. It was my fault for not using my snake-pokin' stick to check the bushes first."

"Mind if I take a look at him?" asked Matthew.

"No sir, I don't mind if he don't."

Buddy allowed Matthew to examine his wound. "You're lucky. Looks like he's gonna make it. If not, he'd already be dead. I only saw a partial fang bite, so the snake probably didn't empty a full load of venom into your dog. Otherwise, he might not have lived. If you gotta be bit by a rattlesnake, the best place is the paw or the face. The venom don't flow as quickly to his heart. You done right tryin' to keep him still."

"Thank you, Mr. Matthew. That's good news."

Buddy licked Matthew's hand.

"You're good with dogs, Mr. Matthew. Buddy likes you. You ever own dogs before?"

"When I was a kid, I did. I like dogs; heck, I even like cats. Not too many of God's creatures I don't like…except snakes. I got a healthy fear of snakes. Everybody in Texas should."

"I sure do, but Buddy is brave. He killed the rattlesnake to save me."

"He's a good dog," said Matthew, softly patting Buddy on the head, "If truth be told, I like dogs better than most people."

Sara Jane's estimation of Matthew's character rose significantly. She knew that people who were kind to animals were good people. Plus, Buddy instinctively knew who he could trust, and he trusted Matthew right away.

Matthew moved back to his corner to give Sara Jane her comfort zone. "So, you like the beach, do you?"

"Yessir. I ain't never been to the ocean, but my daddy was there a long time ago, and he brought me this here seashell." She removed the shell from the sewing tin and handed it to Matthew.

Matthew looked it over and said, "Yep. That's a mighty fine shell." He handed it back to her.

"Thank you. My daddy told me all about the ocean: the waves, the seagulls, the sand, the breeze. I can just picture it in my mind. He was gonna take me there one day, but we never got to go."

"You told me earlier both your parents are dead. How long have you been on your own?"

"My mama died a year ago, and my daddy the year before that. Then I lived with my stepfather, but he's dead now, too."

Matthew, feeling compassion for the girl, sighed and said," Life can sure get lonely without a family. I'm glad you have your dog."

"Do you have any family, Mr. Matthew?"

Matthew paused, then said, "I used to."

"What happened to 'em?"

"I don't know."

Sensing that Matthew was feeling uncomfortable, Sara Jane said no more.

The train slowed down, and Matthew said, "Must be pullin' into Hearne."

CHAPTER 30

THE FISHING CABIN

The next day, Sheriff Black, Deputy Hughes, Jeff Hughes and his dogs, Woody and Guthrie drove to the spot at the river where they left off yesterday.

"Let's take the dogs down the riverbank a bit in case her body was washed downstream," said the sheriff.

Jeff let the dogs smell the dress again. They only walked about 20 yards before they picked up the scent again. The dogs started barking and sped up, pulling Jeff and Mark behind them. The sheriff followed in the pickup.

They walked for about a mile when they came to a bend in the river where an old fishing cabin stood beneath a huge live oak tree.

"That's Eddie Matthew's fishin' cabin," said Deputy Hughes. "He let me use it a coupla times."

"More like a shack," said the sheriff.

"Whatever you call it," said Jeff, "it's a great place to hide out."

They approached the cabin cautiously. Jeff stayed behind with the dogs, who continued sniffing the ground. The sheriff motioned for the deputy to go around the back, then entered the cabin.

After checking out the place, the sheriff called out, "All clear."

The deputy joined him inside, looking around. "Looks pretty clean, like somebody swept away the dust and cobwebs."

"Somebody has definitely been here recently," said the sheriff. "Jeff, bring the dogs in."

Woody and Guthrie sniffed, circled around inside, and began barking.

"Her scent's strong in here, sheriff," said Jeff.

"That's good news. Means she's probably still alive. Wonder why she left?" said the sheriff.

"You still think she's got an adult with her?" asked the deputy.

"Not sure, but if she hasn't been taken, why is she runnin'?" said the sheriff.

They looked around the cabin exterior and came upon the fish cleaning station. "There's blood here," said the sheriff.

"Maybe she cleaned fish and cut herself."

"Hmm," said the sheriff, "either that or an adult did it, which brings us back to the idea that an adult may be traveling with her or took her."

They continued checking the grounds, and Jeff called out, "Look! There's some kind of small wagon wheels leading away from the cabin."

They joined Jeff and looked around. "I only see one set of footprints," said the sheriff. "This just gets more and more confusing. Well, let's get the dogs home and take up here tomorrow."

As the sheriff drove off, he found himself hoping that the wagon was not used to pull the body of a certain young girl.

On the way home, raindrops pelted the truck's windshield. Rain? Where did that come from? As if in answer, the rain fell harder. If this kept up, thought the sheriff, it would be useless to take the dogs out tomorrow. The rain will have washed away any prints, as well as the girl's scent. They'd never be able to track her, if she was even still alive.

CHAPTER 31

RAIN!

Rain! Blessed rain! They had needed rain for so long. The crops and the garden were wilting, and the cracks in the black loam were wide enough to swallow a squirrel. Laura sat in her rocker on the porch petting Methuselah, Queenie lying beside her.

Sam and Hank drove up, and Sam attempted to get out of the truck's broken door. On his third attempt, he succeeded. Hank drove off laughing, spitting tobacco out the window, and for the first time in almost two months, did not leave a trail of dust behind.

Sam cleaned off his boots and shook the rain off his hat before joining Laura on the porch. "Hey, sweetie, nice surprise, huh?"

"It sure is! I think I can hear my garden lapping up the water!"

"I tell you; it came just in time. The crops were starting to wilt. Another couple of weeks without rain might have done us in."

Laura handed Sam a glass of iced tea and said, "Sam, I've been thinking."

Taking the tea, Sam said, "Uh oh, that's never good."

"I'm serious, Sam."

"I'm sorry. What did you want to say?"

"Well," said Laura, "the more I think about it, the more I think the person staying in our barn may have been a child."

"What makes you think that?"

"Queenie, for one. She was genuinely sad the person left, like she had a real bond with them. Also, the innocence of the note and the shelled peas."

"Only children shell peas?"

"No, of course not. It's just such a sweet, child-like thing to do."

"Well, whoever they are, they're gone now, so we don't have to worry about them anymore."

"I just hope it's not a child out there in the rain, all alone."

They stood and walked into the house, Sam's arm around Laura's waist. "Did I ever tell you that you worry way too much?" asked Sam.

"Constantly," said Laura.

CHAPTER 32

MY NAME IS SARA JANE

Sara Jane awoke to the sound of rain on the roof of the metal boxcar. Buddy was sitting up as though on sentry duty. "Hi, Buddy, are you OK?" asked Sara Jane. In response, Buddy licked her hand.

From the darkness, Matthew spoke, "I always love the sound of rain on a metal roof. Haven't heard it in a long time."

"I guess I never heard it before. It's nice. Are we still in Hearne?"

"Yep. As predicted, we'll be in Hearne overnight, then pull out tomorrow."

"Will they be loadin' somethin' in this car?"

"Not this time of year. In the fall it'll be filled with bales of cotton to take to Palestine and places north. But this time of year, it's filled with produce like you see here. When they get to Palestine, they'll unload the produce and fill the car with lumber."

"I guess we'll have to get off before then."

"We'll get off the day before."

"Is it nighttime yet? It's hard to tell from in here."

"Almost. The sun's starting to set. I'm gonna eat somethin'. Would you like half a sandwich?"

"No, thank you, Mr. Matthew. We've got our own food."

There was only the sound of the heavy rain on the roof of the boxcar as they ate in silence.

"If it's Ok, Mr. Matthew, we're gonna lie down now and try to get some sleep."

"Sounds like a good idea," said Matthew, "think I'll do the same."

From across the boxcar, Matthew heard the girl sweetly singing a lullaby to her dog. Then, from the dark, he heard, " Mr. Matthew? Thanks for lettin' us come with you."

"You're welcome, child."

There was a long pause, then, "Mr. Matthew? My name's Sara Jane."

CHAPTER 33

THAT FAMILY CONNECTION

Sheriff Grady Black had a restless night. He usually enjoyed the sound of rain at night, but the thought of the scent being washed away had kept him awake. And, of course, the worst scenario had happened. It had rained hard all night, only slowing down before sunrise, as though a stagehand was calling the cues for the curtain to come down. And yes, this was indeed becoming a drama, a mystery, in fact.

Just as the sheriff poured his coffee, the phone rang. "Sheriff Black"

"Grady? It's Nellie Bell. (Oh, no, it was Nellie Bell callin' at the crack of dawn. Did that woman ever sleep?)

"Yes, Nellie Bell, good mornin'. How can I help you?"

"Well, I'm just calling' to check on your progress in the search for that little girl. I just hate the thought of that child being out there in all this rain."

"Well, if it makes you feel any better, from what I hear, that little girl is pretty smart. I'm sure she found a place to hide from the rain. The good news is the rain has stopped. Also, Jeff Hughes's dogs tracked her scent to a place down by the river. The bad news is the rain probably washed the scent away."

"Well, you can't let that stop you, Grady. Maybe she's hiding out near the place where you last smelled her scent. Have you checked any possible caves or deserted buildings?"

"Yes, Nellie Bell, of course. We think she may have hid at an old fishin' shack for a while, but she was gone when we got there. We're gonna go back there today and check to see if she came back because of the rain. Plus, there's a cave not too terribly far from there."

"I knew you would think of something, Grady. You were always such a smart little boy. Well, I'll let you get to work."

"Nellie Bell, don't tell anyone about all this, OK? This is private sheriff's information," said the sheriff, who had not been a boy for years.

"My lips are sealed, Grady. It's just between the two of us. Good - bye, dear, keep me posted."

Sheriff Black hung up, knowing that Nellie Bell would be on the phone telling everyone she knew. Why did he bother to tell her to be quiet? Gossiping was her greatest joy.

 Oh, well. Maybe he could use this to his advantage. With any luck, she would notify Mr. Conrad, the newspaper editor, and really build up his "heroic" efforts to find the girl. A positive article in the paper could help in an election year.

Sheriff Black took a sip of his now lukewarm coffee. He poured it out and poured a fresh cup from the pot. Nellie Bell could sure get on his last good nerve. At the same time, he knew she had a good heart and was sincerely concerned about the child.

Plus, she had contributed a large amount of money to his campaigns for sheriff, and he owed her. And there was that family connection.

Sheriff Black rinsed out his coffee cup in the sink and headed out.

CHAPTER 34

THE UNWELCOME GUEST

Sara Jane awoke and discovered she was surprisingly rested. Maybe it was the sound of the much-needed rain on the roof of the boxcar, or maybe it was knowing Mr. Matthew was there. In any case, she felt more rested than she had in a long time.

Buddy yawned and stretched.

"Mornin', Mr. Matthew."

"Mornin', Sara Jane. What's your dog's name?"

"Buddy. This here's Buddy. He's been with me as long as I can remember. My daddy gave him to me when I was little. You ever have a dog, Mr. Matthew?"

"When I was a boy. Later on, I had a cat. My wife preferred cats."

"I like cats, too, but there ain't nothin' that loves you as much as a dog."

"You're right about that, Sara Jane."

"You want some breakfast, Mr. Matthew? Buddy and me got some food left."

"That's nice of you, Sara Jane, but I still got half a sandwich."

They ate in silence, then the train started to roll. "Here we go," said Matthew.

"How far do we go before we have to get off?" asked Sara Jane.

"I usually get off about a mile from the Palestine depot. They unload and reload in Palestine, and we don't wanna get caught in the boxcar."

The train started slowing down then came to a stop. That was odd. Matthew peeked through a crack and saw several cows that had gotten loose standing on the tracks. The train blew its whistle, trying to scare the cows off the tracks. Good thing the train had been moving slowly, having just left Hearn.

Matthew sat back down in his corner. Suddenly, the boxcar door partially opened. Matthew and Sara Jane froze. A disheveled man climbed aboard. His clothes were filthy, and Sara Jane could smell the alcohol from where she sat. Buddy growled. The man pulled the door closed.

Not seeing Matthew, who was in the other corner of the boxcar, the man spotted Sara Jane and, slurring his words, said, "Well, well, well. Lookie what we got here. A pretty little girl all by herself. Mind if I sit by you? Been a long time since I seen anyone as pretty as you."

Sara Jane objected, and Buddy growled again, but he sat down beside her anyway, touching one of her pigtails. Sara Jane winced, and Buddy came to attention and growled louder.

From the darkness, Matthew spoke. "The young lady said no, mister. Now be a good fella and step away from her."

"And who are you? Her guardian angel?"

"If need be," said Matthew, crossing closer to the man.

The man swayed and took a drink from an almost empty bottle of whiskey. "You don't scare me, mister. And don't go tellin' me what to do. I just wanna spend some time with this here pretty little girl." He started to sit again, but Matthew stopped him, taking his arm.

"Now I asked you nicely, mister. Get away from the girl now."

Matthew heard the click of a switchblade knife as the man pointed it at him and said, "If you know what's good for you, you'll back off."

Matthew said, "I'm real sorry you had to go and pull a knife on me, mister, 'cause you have crossed a line."

The man lunged at Matthew, who pulled back, barely avoiding the knife blade. Sara Jane yelled, "Get him, Buddy!" Buddy lunged at the man's leg, biting him and holding on for dear life. Matthew then grabbed the man's wrist, twisting until he dropped the knife. The train started moving.

Sara Jane sprang forward and grabbed the knife from the floor while Matthew wrapped his arm around the man's neck and pushed him toward the boxcar door. The train had started to pick up speed.

"OK, Buddy. Let go of his leg," said Matthew. Buddy hesitated and looked at Sara Jane for confirmation before letting go.

"Sara Jane, pull the door open part way." Sara Jane complied, and Matthew pushed the man off the rolling train. The man tumbled down an embankment, and Matthew and Sara Jane pulled the boxcar door shut.

"Good boy, Buddy!" said Matthew, patting Buddy on the head.

"Are you OK, Mr. Matthew?" asked Sara Jane, "Your hand's bleeding."

"I'm OK. Just a little cut from the knife. I'll be fine. Are you OK?"

"I'm fine, thanks to you and Buddy. Let me help you with that cut." Sara Jane had Matthew sit, then brought out her medical supplies and canteen. She washed off the cut, then applied Mercurochrome and wrapped gauze bandage around it.

"Thank you, Sara Jane. That's mighty kind of you. You got all kinds of things in that rucksack, don't you."

"Yessir. You see, Buddy and me decided we had to run away from my stepfather, so we put what we thought we'd need into my rucksack. But there was a terrible accident when he fell and broke the kerosine lamp and caught the house on fire. Buddy and me took off. The house burned down, and he was burned up in it."

"I see," said Matthew. "I'm real sorry." Matthew felt so much compassion for her and wondered why she had felt the need to run away from her stepfather. He hated to even think about what the child had been through.

Sara Jane handed Matthew the knife, and he wiped it off. "Think I'll hang on to this. It might come in handy someday."

"Mr. Matthew," said Sara Jane, "would it be OK if Buddy and me sit closer to you?"

"I would like that," said Matthew, his voice cracking.

CHAPTER 35

YOU COULDN'T HAVE KNOWN

It was midmorning before Sheriff Black arrived back at the fishing shack. He wanted to re-check it in case the girl had used it as shelter from the rain. But the shack was empty, and there were no signs anyone had been in it since they checked it last.

He then drove the pickup about half a mile further, where he knew of a cave on the side of the riverbank. Nothing. And no footprints or wagon wheels. Where could they have gone?

He walked back to the truck and climbed in. He had spotted a white building in the distance. Might as well check it out.

As the wheels of the pickup rolled over the gravel in front of the large farmhouse, a black dog ran out to greet him. Strange, thought the sheriff, the dog isn't barking. Not much of a watchdog. The sheriff walked up the steps to the front porch and knocked on the door. "Hello? Anyone home? It's Sheriff Black."

Laura answered the door, flour on her hands and bibbed apron. She was carrying a cup towel. She had never met the sheriff, but Nellie Bell spoke highly of him, and he had a reputation as a good man.

"Come in, sheriff. I'm Laura Patterson. I'd shake your hand, but ..." she said, indicating her flour-covered hands. "Is everything OK?

Has something happened to my husband?" She rubbed her hands on the cup towel as she asked the sheriff to sit.

Sheriff Black removed his hat as he sat, holding it in his hands between his knees. "Everything's OK, ma'am. I didn't mean to frighten you. I just come by to see if you might have seen a little girl I'm searchin' for. She went missin' a few weeks ago after her family's house burned down. You might have heard about it. You haven't come across her, have ya?"

Laura turned pale. " Oh, that must be the little girl Miss Nellie Bell told me about. She hasn't been found?"

"No, ma'am. We're hopin' she's safe and unharmed, but we haven't been able to find her despite an extensive search. Yesterday, we tracked her to a fishin' shack not too terribly far from here. We found footprints and some small wagon wheels, and it looked like someone had stayed in the shack. We planned to take up the trail today, but the rain washed it away. Your house is the nearest building, so I thought I'd check and see if maybe the girl sought out your house for shelter from the rain."

The minute the sheriff mentioned the wagon wheels, Laura's inner alarm bells went off. "Oh, sheriff. I may have made a terrible mistake. A few days ago, I noticed that someone had been coming into my house and taking food when I was gone. They may have been hiding somewhere on the farm. I didn't think that much of it because we have had several incidents in the past where homeless folk or hobos crossed near our farm on the way to the railroad. We always gave them food."

"What made this different was that this person stayed for a few days and actually came into the house. My husband suggested we leave one more sack of food and a note asking them to leave. I made sure to lock the door when I was gone."

"Did you ever see the person?" asked the sheriff.

"No," said Laura, "but before they left, they left a sweet note."

"You don't by any chance still have it, do you?"

"As a matter of fact, I do. I'll get it for you. I'm not sure why I kept it, but I felt I should." Laura rose and crossed to get the note, which she handed to the sheriff.

The sheriff read the note. "Hmm. Could be a child, but no way to know for sure. Mind if I keep this?"

"And there's something else, sheriff. Along with the note, the person left a bucket of shelled purple hull peas and four nickels. I returned the nickels. I keep thinking that it could have been a child. Do you think it could have been that same little girl?"

"It's possible. Anything else?"

"Yes. Our dog Queenie keeps running into the barn to a spot behind some barrels where the hay is mashed down. Plus, I found some footprints and small wagon wheels headed out of the barn."

"Show me," said the sheriff.

Laura led him to the spot in the barn.

"Yep, looks like a good hidin' place for a child."

"So, you do think it was her?" asked Laura.

"There's a very good chance it was. Especially with those small wagon wheel prints. A small wagon could indicate a child's wagon."

"Oh, I feel terrible! I'm so sorry. The day after the person left, I had a nagging suspicion it had been a child, but I never dreamed it was that same little girl!"

"You couldn't have known," said the sheriff. "How long ago was it she left?"

"Two days, "said Laura.

The sheriff sighed and said, "Do you have any idea which way she headed?"

"Yes, I do. Queenie kept running south down the road a piece, then sitting and staring. I suspect she headed that way. Is that helpful?"

"Yes, ma'am, it sure is. Do this, will ya? Keep an eye out in case she comes back and call me if you think of anything else."

"I sure will, sheriff. And again, I'm really sorry. Let us know if we can help in any way."

"Sure thing. Thank you, ma'am." He started to leave but turned and said, "Oh, by the way. You mentioned Nellie Bell. I'm curious how you know her?"

"Oh," said Laura, "she was best friends with my Great-Aunt Helen, who left us this farm. I've known her since I was a child."

"Interesting, "said the sheriff. Was there anyone in Milam County who didn't know Nellie Bell?

As the sheriff drove off, Laura sat in her rocker and petted Queenie. "Well, Queenie, I really messed up, didn't I?" Queenie licked her hand, and Methuselah, sitting in the other rocker, meowed as if to say, "Don't worry about it."

Now what, thought the sheriff, as he drove away. Where has that child gone? He would hit the trail tomorrow that led south from the farm.

CHAPTER 36

THE HOOVERVILLE

The train stopped in a small town south of Palestine. Sara Jane gathered up her things and disembarked with Matthew's help. Once they were on the ground, she put her rucksack in the wagon and picked up her walking stick. Buddy walked along beside the wagon. Although he was still a bit wobbly, Buddy was brave and tough, so he walked along with a look that said," I don't need no ol' wagon."

"Where we goin' now, Mr. Matthew?"

"We're goin' to a Hooverville I know about. We're gonna stay there a couple of days with some folks I know."

"What's a Hooverville?" asked Sara Jane.

"A Hooverville is a shanty town or tent city," said Matthew. "It's a place where people go when they've lost their homes and have nowhere else to go."

"Why do they call them Hoovervilles?"

"Well, some people call them that because they blame the former president, Herbert Hoover, for the collapse of the economy that caused them to lose their homes."

"Oh," said Sara Jane, who didn't entirely understand. "Are there lots of Hoovervilles?"

"More all the time," said Matthew.

They walked about a mile, then came to a place with lots of pine trees, a short distance from a river. There were tents attached to cars and trucks and tents set between trees, as well as shacks made from wood scraps, metal pieces, tar paper, and anything else that could be found. Sara Jane thought they looked like they could be blown over by the slightest breeze.

A dog ran to greet them. He and Buddy touched noses, circled, and sniffed each other, deciding they would get along just fine. Sara Jane noticed a large cast iron kettle cooking something over a fire made from wood scraps and pine cones. Smoke rose into the air as a woman stirred the pot with a large paddle. Whatever it was smelled good.

Several children ran by, chasing each other and laughing. A man spotted Matthew and called to him, "Hey, Matthew! How are you? Great to see you, my friend."

The short, blonde man shook Matthew's hand. "Good to see you, Alton. This here's Sara Jane and her dog Buddy."

"Welcome, Sara Jane and Buddy." The man led them over to some shade, where they sat down. "Can I get y'all something to drink?"

"Water's fine," said Matthew.

"That all? I got some good moonshine my brother brought me from Kentucky. It'll set your hair on fire," said Alton, laughing.

"No, thanks. I don't drink the hard stuff no more."

Alton left to fetch their drinks.

"He seems like a nice fella," said Sara Jane.

"He is. He and his wife and four kids have been here for more'n two years. I drop by every time I'm out this way and check on them. They lost their farm three years ago. I knew Alton back in Wichita Falls. He saved my life once. I owe him."

Alton brought them each a tin cup full of water. Sara Jane drank from the cup then shared with Buddy.

"How's the family, Alton?" asked Matthew.

"They're good. Had a bit of a scare in January, though. Our youngest caught pneumonia, and we almost lost her, but she's doing fine now. Thelma says come and eat. It's our day to cook, so everybody'll be lined up with their cups. Guests always go first. We're havin' beans," said Alton.

Matthew was reluctant to eat any of the campers' food because they had so little, but he knew that Alton would be offended if he didn't. The truth was those beans sure smelled good. "Thank you, kindly," said Matthew, proffering his tin cup.

"Hello, Matthew," said Alton's wife, Thelma, putting a scoop of beans into his cup. "Who's this pretty little girl you got with you?"

"This here's Sara Jane," said Matthew.

"Welcome, Sara Jane," said Thelma.

"Thank you, ma'am," said Sara Jane, "those beans sure smell good."

After everyone was served, they all sat down in a circle on the ground. Alton introduced his four kids to Sara Jane, then asked that they all bow their heads and hold hands.

"Lord, we thank you for the food you have provided for us. We ask that you bless it to the nourishment of our bodies. In Jesus's name, Amen."

The beans were surprisingly good. It had been a long time since Matthew and Sara Jane had had a hot meal.

After dinner, the men sat around talking while the women cleaned up and the children played. One of Alton and Thelma's daughters, Cynthia, who was around Sara Jane's age, invited her to play with them. Sara Jane was delighted. She couldn't remember the last time she had someone to play with.

"Is it OK, Mr. Matthew?" asked Sara Jane.

"Of course," said Matthew, "have fun." Matthew was touched that the girl had asked permission. What a great kid she was!

"Come on, Buddy!" said Sara Jane.

As soon as the children ran off to play, the men started talking. In earlier days, they would have smoked, but these days, tobacco was a luxury when you sometimes had no food.

"Did you hear about the WPA?" asked Alton.

"Yep. Heard President Roosevelt is hirin' folks to build bridges and buildings for the government to help with the unemployment problem."

"I heard they got some buildin' goin' on in San Antonio and Dallas. I'm thinkin' of hitch-hikin' to Dallas to see if I can get hired on," said Alton.

'Worth a try," said Matthew.

"Who's the little girl you got with you, your granddaughter?" asked Alton.

"I wish she was. She's a great kid. But no, she's a homeless kid whose parents are dead. I met her in Rockdale."

"There's a lot of that these days. Poor kids don't have nobody. Nice of you to help her out," said Alton.

"She's as much help to me as I am to her. Maybe more," said Matthew.

"You got any plans, Matthew?"

"Not really. Just gonna keep travelin' for a while. I'd like to figure out somethin' more permanent for her. A kid needs a place to call home. But so far, I haven't figured it out."

"Sounds like you might just need to pray about it, Matthew. I'll put you in my prayers, as well."

"Thank you, Alton."

That night, Matthew offered Sara Jane his bedroll, but she declined, saying she had her quilt. "Mr. Matthew? Can we sleep closer to the river? It's so peaceful."

"Sounds good," said Matthew.

The soothing sound of the river, the night critter symphony, the slight breeze, and the fragrance of the pine trees helped Sara Jane fall asleep quickly.

When she awoke the next morning, she spotted Matthew sitting a little further off on the riverbank, deep in thought. She crossed to him and said, "You OK, Mr. Matthew?"

"Oh, mornin', Sara Jane. I'm fine, just gotta lot on my mind. You ever skip stones in the river?"

"No sir, can you show me?" asked Sara Jane.

" Sure thing. First, you gotta find a small, smooth stone," said Matthew.

"Like David," said Sara Jane.

"David?" asked Matthew.

"Yes. David and Goliath in the Bible," said Sara Jane.

Matthew smiled and said, "Of course; I wasn't thinking. OK, take your stone and hold your wrist kind of sideways. Then throw the stone like you want it to skim across the top of the water."

Matthew watched as she skimmed one stone after another across the water. Buddy barked and wagged his tail, wanting to participate.

"Thank you, Mr. Matthew. I love this!"

They sat back down in their sleeping area and ate what was left of Sara Jane's food, which, of course, she shared with Buddy then they walked back to the camp.

"We gotta few beans left in the pot, if you're hungry," said Thelma. "Won't be another meal until this evenin', when the Thompson's are makin' stew. The men are out huntin' squirrels and rabbits for the stew. If they don't catch any, we'll try for some fish."

"Sara Jane, think we can help out with that stew?" said Matthew.

Sara Jane smiled and said, "Yes, sir, I believe we can." She opened her rucksack and removed six large carrots, five onions, and six large potatoes, then handed them to Thelma.

"Oh, my Lord!" exclaimed Thelma. "Where on earth did you get all that?"

"We rode here in a boxcar carrying produce to Palestine. Thought you could use some," said Matthew.

Thelma teared up and said, "We ain't seen vegetables like this in a long time. All we got growin' now is some pitiful, wilted lettuce we was gonna put in the stew tonight. Hadn't had enough rain to grow much of anything lately. Wait 'til Mabel Thompson sees all this; we're gonna have the best stew we've had in a long time!"

"Might have some rain headed up this way. We had a downpour in Milam County the other day," said Matthew.

"We'll keep our fingers crossed and say a prayer, too. Sara Jane, we're mighty grateful for the produce. Cynthia is over by the red tent making paper dolls out of old newspapers if you'd like to join her," added Thelma.

"Go have fun, Sara Jane," said Matthew. Buddy happily trotted along behind her, anxious to play with their dog they called Shep.

"That's a real sweet girl, Matthew. Alton told me about her loss. Sure glad she found you," said Thelma.

"And I'm glad I found her," said Matthew. "Anything I can help you with, Thelma?"

"As a matter of fact, there is. If you don't mind doin' woman's work. Let's take these vegetables over to Mable's and cut 'em up for the stew."

They loaded up, grabbed a couple of knives, and headed over to Mable's tent. "Hey, Mabel! You're not gonna believe what we got for ya!" said Thelma, smiling.

Matthew wasn't the greatest peeler and chopper due to his one hand missing a couple of fingers, but he managed OK, although he was a bit slow. He glanced over and saw Cynthia and Sara Jane happily playing, and it warmed his heart.

As he chopped the vegetables, Matthew realized that his few days with Sara Jane had been the happiest days he'd had in a very long time. She had touched his heart and renewed his spirit. Had he been sent to her, or had she been sent to him? Either way, Matthew thanked God for her.

That evening, the folks in the Hooverville enjoyed the best stew they'd had in a very long time. In addition to the vegetables, the men had provided three rabbits and a squirrel. There was even enough left over to provide tomorrow's supper, as well.

The next morning, Matthew and Sara Jane reluctantly packed their gear and prepared to leave. Matthew explained to Sara Jane that he didn't like to stay more than a couple of days and take advantage of their kindness and generosity.

Sara Jane hugged Cynthia and whispered, "I'll never forget you." She handed her something wrapped in a cloth. "Don't open it 'til we're gone," she said.

Matthew thanked Alton and Thelma and promised to stop by again soon.

As soon as they were out of sight, Cynthia opened the cloth and found Sara Jane's last four nickels.

CHAPTER 37

THE LOST FAMILY

Matthew and Sara Jane made their way to the nearest railroad but were dismayed to see two bulls with clubs guarding the freight cars.

"Bulls," said Matthew, who had stopped walking.

"Bulls?" asked Sara Jane.

"Bulls are men with clubs hired by the railroad company to keep people off the freight trains. Don't worry. I recognize one of 'em, and I still have enough money to pay them off."

They approached the men who yelled at them to keep away, then one of the men recognized Matthew.

"That you, Matthew? I didn't recognize you with the kid."

"Hey, George. We're headed west for a bit. Can you help us out?" asked Matthew, who held out two one-dollar bills.

"Sure thing, Matthew," said George. He approached the other man and handed him one of the dollars. They stepped back and allowed Matthew, Sara Jane, and Buddy to climb aboard the boxcar.

"Thanks, George. See ya next time," said Matthew.

"Safe travels, Matthew."

After they settled down in the boxcar, Sara Jane asked, "Where we goin' now, Mr. Matthew?"

"Well, we're heading west, but I haven't quite decided where we'll get off next."

"Mr. Matthew, I sure liked Cynthia and her family. They're good people."

"They sure are. I admire how they always stay hopeful and positive, even though they don't have anything," said Matthew.

"Oh, but they do, Mr. Matthew," said Sara Jane, "they have each other."

Matthew teared up, glad it was dark inside the boxcar and Sara Jane couldn't see him clearly. "You're right, Sara Jane. Family is the most important thing of all."

Sara Jane said, "They also have Jesus, and that's even more important."

Matthew could not disagree.

About a half hour later, the train started to move. They sat in silence for a while, and Sara Jane noticed a faraway look on Matthew's face when the sunlight from one of the cracks in the boxcar passed over his face.

"You gotta lot on your mind, Mr. Matthew?"

"Yes, I do. I been thinkin' a lot about my family," said Matthew.

"You think they are still alive?" asked Sara Jane.

"I sure hope so," said Matthew.

"You thinkin' of lookin' for 'em?"

"I don't know. I'd like to, but I don't think they'd want to see me," said Matthew.

"Why not?" asked Sara Jane.

Matthew sighed, paused, then said," Because I done somethin' real bad. I run off and left 'em when they needed me."

"Oh," said Sara Jane, "Why'd you do that?"

Matthew sighed again and said, "It's hard to explain, but at the time, I was a broken man. I'd lost my job with the railroad after I got injured at work and couldn't do the job no more. I was in worse shape than I am now, and I couldn't find work to support my family. I was already feeling like a failure, then I found out my wife had started seein' my boss, and it just broke me. I started drinkin'. I turned to the bottle instead of the Lord.

I finally decided I was useless to my family and might even be draggin' them down. Feelin' like they were better off without me, I left them a note, then walked away and never looked back. That was eight years ago."

There was only silence, then Matthew continued, "For years I just wandered, the weight of the world on my shoulders, drinkin' to soothe the pain and guilt, feelin' unworthy of forgiveness."

When Matthew finished, a soft-spoken Sara Jane said, "Mr. Matthew, there ain't nuthin' a person could do that is so bad that Jesus won't forgive him."

"I know that now, Sara Jane. About a year ago, me and a coupla drinkin' buddies was ridin' the rails and stopped near one of them tent revivals. We weren't as hungry for The Word as we were for the soup they served after the service.

Now I have been to a few of these before. I sang the hymns and said the prayers without any feeling, then ate the soup and went on my way.

But for some reason, things were different that night. I can't explain it, but somehow it was like I heard the words for the first time. Maybe it was how that particular preacher spoke, I don't know, but for the first time in my life, I understood Jesus's message of love and forgiveness.

When there was an altar call at the end of the service, I walked forward and received the preacher's blessing. After the crowd dispersed and my buddies left, the preacher sat with me, and we talked for a long time. He told me what you just told me, Sara Jane. I asked him to baptize me, and he did, right there on the spot. I felt the weight of guilt lift from my shoulders and my heart.

I was never the same after that. I still rode the rails, but I quit drinkin' and got myself together. I stopped thinkin' only of myself and all my troubles.

As I traveled, I started gettin' a little work where I could and tried to help others along the way, but I still haven't gotten up the nerve to search for my family and ask for their forgiveness."

After a long pause, Sara Jane said, "But Mr. Matthew, if Jesus forgave you, why wouldn't your family?"

"Because Jesus didn't have to experience me as a husband and a father. I can't imagine my family being willin' to forgive me or wantin' to see me."

"Ask Jesus to guide you and walk with you, Mr. Matthew. He'll give you the strength to do it. Plus, Buddy and I will go with you for support," said Sara Jane.

Matthew smiled, "Thank you, Sara Jane. Let me mull it over and pray on it a while."

Matthew was amazed at the effect this child had on him. Except for the tent revival preacher, Matthew had never revealed his story to anyone.

That night, Matthew turned his troubles over to God, and woke up with a feeling of calm and determination. He knew that he would never find peace until he found his family and asked for their forgiveness.

"Sara Jane, I'm finally at peace about all this. It feels like the right thing to do. Let's go to Fort Worth and look for my family."

"I'm so glad, Mr. Matthew." Buddy started wagging his tail and smiling. "Look! Buddy's excited."

They were in a boxcar in a train heading to Dallas and would need to get off there and take a different train to Fort Worth, which was further west. There was little conversation along the way. Sara Jane sensed that Matthew needed the quiet to help him process his thoughts and feelings. This was a huge step for him, and she knew it would take courage to face a family he had once abandoned. She was proud of him for taking this step.

What awaited him? Would they still be in Fort Worth? If so, how would they receive him? Would they reject him or welcome him? Were they even still alive?" Sara Jane said a silent prayer that the meeting would go well. Whatever the outcome, she and Buddy would be there for him.

CHAPTER 38

WISH I'D KNOWN HIM

"Stop beating yourself up over this, sweetheart. Neither of us could have known it was her," said Sam.

"Realistically, I know this. I just keep thinking that I should have gone with my gut the day she left and called the sheriff."

"Laura, no one blames you for any of this, not even Miss Nellie Bell. No one even knew if the girl was alive or where she might be."

"I just have so many questions. Is she by herself, or has some stranger taken her? If she's by herself, why is she running? Is she afraid her stepfather is still alive? Why is she afraid of him? Whatever the situation, she must be terrified."

"Laura, the sheriff will take care of things. Do what you always tell me to do, turn it over to God."

Laura sighed and said, "You're right, Sam. I've given this way too much thought and emotion. My father used to say, 'Never worry about something you can't do anything about.'"

"A very wise man. I'm sorry I never got to meet him."

"Me, too. He would have loved you."

"I do have some good news," said Laura. "Pastor Chris called and asked me to teach the children's Sunday School class. I start this Sunday."

"That's great!" said Sam. "You'll be a great teacher. They are lucky to have you."

"And I am blessed to have them."

"I have some good news, too," said Sam, "Hank finally got that broken pickup door fixed."

"No! How on earth did you get him to finally do it?" said Laura.

"It wasn't me; it was Velma. Last Sunday, he drove Velma to church. He hit a pothole, the broken door flew open, and Velma bounced right out of the open door onto the ground. To make matters worse, the pothole was muddy from the rain we had."

"Oh, no! Was Velma hurt?"

"Only her pride. Hank said she had plenty of padding if you know what I mean."

Laura laughed and said, "I know I shouldn't laugh, but that is funny!"

"Hank said he had no idea Velma could curse. He said she let out a string of cuss words that could curl your teeth. Later on, she claimed she wasn't cursing, but speaking in tongues, but Hank said he recognized several very familiar cuss words."

Still laughing, Laura said, "No wonder the door got fixed. Oh, Sam, you always know how to cheer me up."

"You know what will cheer me up?"

"What?" asked Laura with a coy smile.

"If you get that cornbread out of the oven before it burns."

"Oh, no! The cornbread!" said Laura, running into the kitchen.

Sam just laughed and shook his head.

CHAPTER 39

THE TRAIN DEPOT

Sheriff Black and Deputy Hughes stopped by Jeff's place to pick up him and the dogs, Woody and Guthrie. The rain had washed away the old trail, but after speaking to Laura Patterson, they hoped there might be a new trail heading south from the Patterson farm. It was worth a try, especially since they had no other leads.

When they arrived a half mile south of the Patterson farm, they let the dogs smell the dress again and began walking south. After a quarter of a mile, the dogs picked up the scent and began circling and barking. Mark and Jeff each took a leash and followed the dogs while Sheriff Black went back for the pickup truck.

They had walked a mile when they reached the railroad track.

"You don't think she hopped a freight train, do you?" asked Deputy Hughes.

"Not by herself," said Sheriff Black, looking worried. "But then again, nothin' that child has done seems like somethin' a nine-year-old girl would do. In any case, the scent hasn't stopped, so if she did hop a freight, it was in Rockdale. Let's keep goin'. With any luck, she might still be there."

They followed the scent to the Rainbow Courts. Sheriff Black knocked on the manager's office. "Howdy, ma'am. I'm Sheriff Grady Black."

"I know who you are, sheriff. How can I help you?" said Cindy Jones, the owner.

"We're lookin' for a little girl who disappeared a few weeks ago. We have reason to believe she may have been here recently. Haven't seen her, have you?" said the sheriff.

"That the little girl in the paper? The one whose house burned down?" asked Cindy.

"Yes'm, that's the one."

"No, Sheriff Black, the only child that's been here in the past couple of days is a boy who was stayin' with his folks."

"Both parents, mom and dad?" asked the Sheriff.

"Yessir. They're from San Antonio. They've stayed here before. Got family in Dallas," said Cindy.

"I see. Well, if she shows up or you think of anything, give me a call," said the sheriff.

"Sure will, Sheriff Black. Good luck with your search."

While Sheriff Black had been questioning the owner, Deputy Hughes and his brother had continued following the dogs around the property.

"She may have just stopped here to rest. The trail leads to those trees, which explains how she could have been here and not been seen," said Deputy Hughes.

"Where does the trail lead after that?" asked the sheriff.

"It leads away from here, toward town," said the deputy.

"Well," said the sheriff, "Let's get goin'; we're burnin' daylight."

They followed the dogs to the train depot, and the scent stopped there.

"Well, Mark, your idea about her hoppin' a freight train just may have been accurate. I'll question the people workin' here," said the sheriff. "Why don't you two take the dogs and continue searchin' the grounds in case the scent takes up again."

The sheriff walked up the steps of the depot and was greeted by Charles Young, who managed the depot. "Howdy, sheriff. What can I help you with?"

"Hey, Charles. We're lookin' for a little girl who went missin' a few weeks ago. You may have heard about her."

"The one in the paper? No, haven't seen her."

"She might have had a man and a dog travelin' with her."

"No, I would have for sure noticed that. The dog wouldn't have been allowed on the train," said Charles.

"What about a freight train? Could they have sneaked on?" asked the sheriff.

"No way. We keep alert for that kind of thing. The railroad frowns on it."

"Anyone else work here when you're off duty?" asked the sheriff.

"Just my nephew Fred," said Charles. "Want to talk to him?"

"Probably a good thing. Wanna cover all our bases," said the sheriff.

"Hold on, he's inside," said Charles. A minute later, Charles came back out with a very nervous young man. "Sheriff, this here's Fred. Ask him anything you need to."

"Much obliged, Charles," said the sheriff. "Do you mind stayin' here while I interview Fred?"

"Sure thing, sheriff," said Charles.

"Fred, you happen to know anything about a little girl sneakin' on the freight train? Might of been with a man and a dog," said the sheriff.

By this point, Fred was starting to turn pale and sweat profusely. He had trouble standing in place.

"Fred," said his uncle, if you know anything, you best speak up."

"Yessir, I seen a girl with a man and a dog. I let 'em sneak onto a boxcar," said Fred.

"You what?" said Charles.

"I'm sorry, Uncle Charles, but they paid me a dollar a piece, and I really needed the money. I didn't think it would hurt anything."

"Fred, that little girl was the one everybody's lookin' for!" said Charles.

"I'm sorry; I didn't know that," said Fred.

"What about the man she was with? Did she seem afraid of him?' asked the sheriff.

"No, sir. I know the man. His name's Matthew. He comes through Rockdale from time to time. He's a real nice guy. She didn't seem afraid of him at all."

"Where was their train headin', Fred," asked the sheriff.

"It was headed to Hearne, but I don't know where after that," said Fred. "Look, I thought the girl was his granddaughter or something. She seemed comfortable with him, not like he was takin' her against her will or anything."

"I still don't like the idea of a young girl travelin' with some drifter, no matter how nice he seemed," said the sheriff.

"Sheriff," said Charles, "I'm sure sorry about all this. I'll file a report with the railroad and get notification out to neighborin' towns."

"Thank you, Charles," said the sheriff.

"And YOU! Start lookin' for another job. You're fired! I don't care if your mother is my sister," said Charles.

"But Uncle Charles, I said I was sorry! I won't do it again," said Fred as he followed his uncle inside.

Families, thought Sheriff Black as he walked down the depot steps.

Deputy Hughes and Jeff had finished searching the grounds and had overheard the last part of the conversation.

"I take it we don't need to search any further here," said Mark.

"Nope. Mark, drop me off at the office, then take Jeff and the dogs home. We won't be needin' them anymore. Jeff, I sure thank you for your help. We wouldn't have figured any of this out without you. I owe you one," said the sheriff.

"Glad I could be of help," said Jeff.

 After the sheriff was dropped off at his office, he went inside and plopped down in his desk chair. He could sure use a drink, but that would have to wait until he got home. For now, he needed to start contacting sheriffs in nearby counties.

The kid was ridin' the rails and had an adult with her. She could be anywhere. The bulletins he would put out would alert law enforcement to be on the lookout. Hopefully, the further away from home they got, the less careful they would be.

Realistically, it was like a needle in a haystack. They could get off the train anywhere along the line. More and more Hoovervilles were appearing, and they could easily hide in one of those.

Sheriff Black decided to make one stop before going home. He needed to update Miss Nellie Bell in person before word got out about the latest development. It wouldn't surprise him, though, if she already knew.

CHAPTER 40

THE CHINA TEACUP

After leaving the train in Fort Worth, Matthew found a filling station that had sandwiches for sale. He only had one dollar left, but it paid for one sandwich with 80 cents change. He would share the sandwich with Sara Jane.

After eating, Matthew and Sara Jane cleaned up a little in the filling station bathroom, which they were allowed to use since they had made a purchase. It felt wonderful being able to wash his face and clean his body with a cloth. He couldn't do much about his long hair or dirty clothes, but this was better than nothing.

They walked about an hour until they came to a small brick house in a nice but modest neighborhood. The house was red brick with a dark roof and white shutters and doors. The house was nice, but time had not been kind to it. In fact, most houses in the neighborhood showed signs of neglect, a symptom of a bad economy.

Matthew stopped at the bottom of the sidewalk. There was a long pause, then Sara Jane said, "Is this your house, Mr. Matthew?"

"It was," said Matthew, still hesitating.

"It's nice, Mr. Matthew."

After a long pause, Sara Jane added, "I know you're nervous, Mr. Matthew, but Buddy and me are with you. I bet your family is inside and will be so excited to see you!"

Matthew knew that taking this next step would change his life one way or another. He summoned his courage, said a silent prayer, and walked to the front door, Sara Jane and Buddy following.

Matthew knocked on the door and removed his hat. A woman he didn't know answered the door. "Yes?" asked the woman.

"Excuse me, ma'am. I'm lookin' for my family who used to live here. The name's Layne, Matthew Layne."

"Sorry. I don't know the people who used to live here. We've lived here six years. The house was abandoned when we bought it. You might check with Brenda Burks down the street. She's in the yellow house. She's lived there most of her life. She might know something."

"Much obliged," said Matthew.

"Oh, wait!" said the woman. "You might not be interested in this, but I found something when we moved into the house. I'll get it for you."

When she returned, she handed Matthew a child's China teacup. "I thought it might have special meaning."

Holding the teacup, Matthew teared up. It had belonged to his girls.

"Thank you, ma'am'. I appreciate your thoughtfulness."

Matthew put on his hat then handed the precious teacup to Sara Jane. "Will you hold on to this, Sara Jane? It belonged to my girls."

"Yes, Mr. Matthew. I'll take good care of it for you."

They crossed to the yellow house, Matthew once again removing his hat when he knocked.

A woman opened the door. "Yes? Can I help you?"

"Brenda," said Matthew, "You probably don't recognize me, but I'm Matthew Layne. Do you remember me?"

"Oh, my Lord! As I live and breathe! I thought you were dead. And, of course, I remember you, Matthew. I remember you left your family," said Brenda.

"Not something I'm proud of, Brenda," said Matthew, twisting the brim of his hat in his hands. "I'm lookin' for them. Any idea where they went? I don't mean 'em no harm. I want to make amends."

Brenda stood there, a frown on her face, then noticing Sara Jane, she said, "Come on in, Matthew. You and the girl. The dog has to stay out here. I'll tell you what I know."

CHAPTER 41

UPDATING NELLIE BELL

Sheriff Grady Black knocked on Miss Nellie Bell's door and was welcomed by Ezelle. "Come on in, Sheriff Black, Miss Nelle Bell is in the parlor. She just finished her supper. Can I get something for you?"

"No, thank you, Ezelle, I won't be long."

She escorted him into the parlor and said, "Look who's come to see ya, Miss Nellie Bell!"

Sheriff Black removed his Stetson when he walked into the room.

"Hello, Grady! I hope you have some good news for me," said Nellie Bell.

"Yes and no," said the sheriff, as he sat, hat in his hands. "We tracked the little girl usin' a dress of hers we found in her treehouse and Jeff Hughes's bloodhounds. We followed the scent along the riverbank for a long time. We know she spent some time in an old fishin' shack, and we believe she spent several days hidin' on the Patterson farm."

"Sam and Laura's place? Why didn't they tell someone?" asked Nellie Bell.

"They didn't know until the person was gone. The rain washed away some of the trail, but we managed to trace her to the train depot in Rockdale."

"The train depot!" said Miss Nellie incredulously.

"Yes. Upon questionin' the employees, we were able to get one man to admit he had allowed the girl, her dog, and an adult male to sneak on a boxcar headed for Hearne."

"Oh, no! Did he know who the man was?"

"Only that he was a drifter named Matthew. He said the man came through Rockdale from time to time and seemed like a nice guy."

"Well, I don't like the sound of that. What if the man kidnapped her?"

"We thought of that, but the employee said she seemed to be with him of her own free will," said the sheriff.

"I sure hope so. Oh, this is just so frustrating!" said Nellie Bell.

"I know. I sent bulletins to law enforcement in nearby counties, and Charles at the train depot is alerting railroad stations. For now, that's all we can do," said the sheriff.

"Thank you, Grady. All we can do now is pray for her safety. Have you eaten yet, Grady? You've been so busy I don't see how you've had time."

"You're right. I haven't, but I can grab somethin' at home," said the sheriff.

"Now, Grady, that just won't do. You have to keep up your strength. Ezelle! Will you please fix the sheriff a plate? It's chicken and dumplings, Grady. And fried okra."

"Yes'm. Sure will." replied Ezelle.

As much as the sheriff just wanted to go home, the thought of a hot meal sure sounded good. And Ezelle was a wonderful cook. The sheriff relented with gratitude.

"Make yourself comfortable, Grady. And pour yourself a shot of brandy. After a day like today, I'm sure you need it."

Sheriff Black had to hand it to Nellie Bell; sometimes she knew just the right thing to do.

CHAPTER 42

THAT'S ALL I KNOW

Matthew and Sara Jane followed Brenda into the kitchen. She had them sit at the small kitchen table and brought them both a glass of lemonade that they eagerly drank.

"I don't know for sure where your family is, but I do know a few things. After you left, your wife continued seein' that man she had taken up with…your boss, if I remember correctly. After a few months, he left her. Word has it he took up with some other woman.

Your wife started takin' in washin', ironin', and sewin'. Your girls helped her. She came close to losin' the house but managed to avoid foreclosure for a couple of years. Then your older girl got married to a fella from Oklahoma and moved back there with him. Not the smartest thing to do, if you ask me, considerin' the situation there.

Your wife and younger daughter lived here another year or so until your younger met and married a young man from Dallas and moved there. His family had a small farm and ferrier business.

By then, your wife had lost the house. Your younger daughter wanted your wife to move in with them, but she decided to move to Oklahoma to live with your older daughter. I didn't hear from them after that." There was a long pause.

"I'm sorry, Matthew. That's all I know," said Brenda.

"Thank you, Brenda. It's a lot more than I knew before," said Matthew. There was another long pause.

"We thought you were dead, Matthew," said Brenda.

"There was a time I wished I was," said Matthew quietly.

Matthew stood and pushed back the kitchen chair. "Thanks again, Brenda. We best be on our way."

"Oh, one more thing, Matthew. I don't know for sure if it's true, but I heard your younger daughter and her husband moved to somewhere in Milam County. Somethin' about inheriting some property."

"Thank you, Brenda. That's very helpful," said Matthew.

Brenda escorted them to the door. "Good luck, Matthew. Here's a little something in case you get hungry later." She handed a small package to Sara Jane, who thanked her.

Matthew's head was spinning. He wasn't sure what to feel. There was too much information to process, yet not enough. There wasn't much chance he could find his wife and older daughter in Oklahoma. Things had been chaotic there for several years now.

But if his hunch was right, he just might know where to find his younger daughter. The one who had always had his heart, his sweet Laura.

CHAPTER 43

THE BULLS

Matthew, Sara Jane, and Buddy caught a freight train headed for Dallas, then switched to one headed south to Waco. Matthew had been deep in thought after his visit to Fort Worth, and Sara Jane had remained quiet so he could deal with whatever was on his mind.

"Mr. Matthew, I'm sorry your family wasn't still in Fort Worth. But that lady said one of your daughters might be in Milam County. That's where I used to live, isn't it?"

"Yes, it is. We're headed to Waco now. We'll find someplace to rest, then head down to Rockdale. I know someone there who might know where my daughter is," said Matthew.

"That's good, Mr. Matthew. That's real good."

About two miles north of Waco, the train slowed down unexpectedly then came to a stop. Matthew peeked through a crack and saw a couple of bulls with clubs checking each boxcar. He didn't recognize either of them and had not expected to be stopped there. All he could do was wait for them to reach their car, which was only two more boxcars away.

"Sara Jane," said Matthew, "Get your things together and be prepared to get off here. There are two bulls who are gonna check this car any minute now. I don't know either of them, and I don't have any more money to pay them off."

The men arrived at their boxcar and banged on the side of it. Then they opened the side door, saw Matthew, Sara Jane, and Buddy, and yelled, "Everybody out! You can't be in here. Now get down."

After they got out of the car, one of the bulls said, "Now go on. I don't wanna see either of you on this train again!" The man hit Matthew hard on the back with the club, causing him to stumble and fall to his knees. Buddy growled and started to lunge at the man, but Sara Jane grabbed Buddy, held him tight, and said, "No, Buddy. Stay."

Sara Jane was angry and scared and had tears in her eyes, but she had the sense to not allow Buddy to attack the man for fear he would kill or severely hurt her beloved dog. The man stood there with his club held up, staring at her and Buddy. "Why do you have to be so mean, mister? We weren't hurting anything." Tears poured down her cheeks.

Seeing this, the other bull said, "Come on, Dennis, you made your point. They're leavin'."

Dennis put down the club and followed the other man to the next boxcar.

Sara Jane and Buddy crossed to Matthew, who was slowly getting up. "You OK, Mr. Matthew?"

"I'm fine, Sara Jane. You were very brave speakin' up like that."

"I just don't get it, Mr. Matthew. Why did he hit you? We were doin' what he told us to do."

"Sara Jane, some people are just filled with rage for some reason we can't possibly know. That man could have just suffered a terrible personal loss or be ashamed that he couldn't provide for his family. Times are hard these days. Maybe under ordinary circumstances, he wouldn't have done that. It's best not to engage with people like that when they have the upper hand," said Matthew.

"OK, Mr. Matthew, I'll try to understand."

"Buddy," said Matthew, I appreciate how you wanted to come to my aid. You're a good dog," He patted Buddy on the head, and Buddy licked his hand.

"Sara Jane, it's gettin' late in the day, and I don't want us to be walkin' in the dark. Let's find a spot to spend the night, then finish walkin' to Waco tomorrow."

"OK, Mr. Matthew."

Matthew was exhausted and aching all over. He knew Sara Jane must be tired, as well.

CHAPTER 44

THE BOBCAT

They walked away from the railroad tracks until they came to a large outcropping of rocks surrounded by some foliage that would provide shelter. They used the walking stick to check the area for snakes, then dropped their gear at the bottom of a particularly large boulder and cleared out an area to sit.

"Are you OK, Mr. Matthew? That man hit you real hard," said Sara Jane.

"I'm OK, Sara Jane, just a little sore is all. Why don't you and Buddy rest here while I gather some firewood. When it gets dark, we'll need a fire to keep away critters and mosquitoes. Mind if I take your wagon?"

"Don't you need help, Mr. Matthew?"

"No, I only need enough for a small fire. You need to rest. It's been a hard day. And Sara Jane, don't stray too far from the campsite, OK?"

"OK, Mr. Matthew."

While Matthew gathered wood, Sara Jane opened her rucksack and pulled out her canteen, the tin cup and bowl, and her quilt, which lay on the ground. She and Buddy sat on it and rested. As she looked around, Sara Jane said, "It's really pretty here, isn't it, Buddy? I love all the big rocks. If you look further off, you can even see some hills. We don't have hills like that back home. I sure would like to climb those. The trees are different, too. I recognize the cactus, but I wonder what kind of tree that is? It's all spiky and kind of short for a tree. I'll ask Mr. Matthew when he gets back."

Sara Jane heard twigs snapping, and Buddy barked, announcing Matthew's arrival. He had the wagon about half full of branches and twigs. "You still got those matches, Sara Jane? You were smart to bring them. I got a couple of flints, but matches are quicker."

Sara Jane handed the matches to Matthew, who soon had a nice fire going just as it grew dark. "That wood smells good, Mr. Matthew? What kind of wood is that?"

"There are a couple of different kinds of wood, but the kind you smell is mesquite. I like the smell, too. It comes from the trees like that over there," said Matthew.

"Oh, I wondered what kind of tree that was." Sara Jane opened the package Brenda had given them, "Look here, Mr. Matthew, that lady gave us two rolls and some cheese!"

As they shared the last of their food, both Matthew and Sara Jane were grateful for the kindness of so many people. "Give us this day, our daily bread," said Matthew.

"I know that. It's from the Lord's Prayer, isn't it, Mr. Matthew," said Sara Jane.

"Sure is. The Lord has sure been providin' for us, hasn't he?" said Matthew. "We need to make sure we are always grateful."

"Yes, Mr. Matthew."

"Well, it's gettin late. Let's get some sleep so we can get an early start walkin' to Waco in the mornin.'"

As Matthew lay on his bedroll, he had trouble sleeping. He ached all over, not just from the hit from the bull's club but also from his bad leg and foot. They had walked a lot that day, and he was dreading having to walk further tomorrow. The thought of finding his daughter, however, made it all worth it.

They were awakened by the sound of Buddy furiously barking. It was not sunrise yet.

The light was still faint. Then they heard it: the heart-stopping sound of a large cat of some kind on the boulder right above them.

Buddy ran around the back of the boulder and up to the top and stood furiously barking, the hair on the back of his neck standing straight up. The cat attacked Buddy, biting and clawing. Sara Jane ran around back and up to the top as Matthew grabbed the walking stick and yelled, "Sara Jane, don't!"

Sara Jane ran toward the cat, throwing rocks at it, trying to make the furious cat leave Buddy alone. She managed to get between them, and the cat lit into her with a vengeance, clawing and biting. By this time, Matthew, slowed down by his bad leg and foot, reached the cat, who was again attacked by Buddy. Matthew stepped forward and whacked the cat with several hard hits with the walking stick. The cat, stunned, fell down, and Matthew lunged forward with the switchblade knife, stabbing it into the cat's neck, killing it.

Sara Jane and Buddy lay on the ground, bleeding from their wounds. It was then that Matthew noticed the fire had gone out. This was his fault, he thought. He should have kept the fire going, but exhausted, he had finally fallen asleep.

With great difficulty, Matthew kneeled to check on Sara Jane and Buddy. Sara Jane sat up and tenderly stroked Buddy, who lay panting and bleeding from the scratches and bites.

"Oh, Buddy! You are so brave. I'm sorry I couldn't help more. You'll be OK. Mr. Matthew and I will take care of you," said Sara Jane, tears rolling down her cheeks. Buddy whined and continued panting.

Matthew thought his heart would break. Sara Jane had blood running down her face, neck, and arms, yet all she could think of was saving her dog. He helped her up and said softly, "Sara Jane, you need help. We need to go. Let me help you back down to the ground, then I'll come back for Buddy."

With great effort, Matthew helped Sara Jane sit down on her quilt. He then went back to the top of the boulder and carried Buddy down, putting him next to Sara Jane. He opened Sara Jane's rucksack, removing the canteen and medical supplies. He poured water over a cloth, washed off her wounds, and applied Mercurochrome, causing her to cry out. She had extensive scratches on her arms, face, and neck. Her overalls had protected her legs, but there were deep claw marks on her ankles. He pressed the cloth firmly on one of the ankle wounds that continued to bleed and held it there until the bleeding stopped.

Matthew then washed Buddy's wounds and, at Sara Jane's insistence, applied Mercurochrome, not knowing if it helped a dog or not.

Matthew then gave Sara Jane and Buddy a drink of water, and took a drink himself. He started packing up their gear.

"Sara Jane, we're gonna rest here a few minutes, then we have to leave and get help. We can't stay here. I'm gonna put you in the wagon and put your rucksack in your lap. We're gonna walk until we find a crossroads up ahead and try to get someone to stop and help us."

"But what about Buddy? We can't just leave him here to die?" said Sara Jane in tears.

"I don't know what else to do, Sara Jane, I can't pull the wagon with you in it and carry Buddy at the same time. Maybe we could get help for you, then come back for him," said Matthew.

"No, no! I won't leave him. He would never leave me. I'm OK, Mr. Matthew. I can walk, and we can put Buddy in the wagon with my rucksack."

Matthew knew there was no arguing with her, so they laid the quilt in the wagon and put Buddy on it. The rucksack, however, would not fit, so Matthew lifted it onto his miserably sore back, along with his own bedroll.

They made their way down the way, both Matthew and Sara Jane walking in pain. Matthew noticed that Sara Jane was faltering, but she wouldn't dare stop for fear Matthew would put her in the wagon and leave Buddy behind.

The sun had come up fully as they reached a crossroads. They had walked only a mile, but it seemed much further. Suddenly, Sara Jane collapsed. Mathew dropped the gear and leaned down to help her. She had completely passed out.

Just then, a car carrying several people spotted them and pulled over to help.

"You need help, mister?" asked the driver.

"Yes, I do. I need to get help for this little girl and her dog. They were attacked by a bobcat," said Matthew.

The man leaned his head out the window and looked at Sara Jane and Buddy. "Look, as you can see, my car is packed full of people. Got a wife and four kids. We can squeeze the little girl into the back, but we ain't got room for you and the dog and your stuff."

Matthew knew Sara Jane would hate this, and he didn't like the idea of putting her in a car with strangers.

"I can't do that," said Matthew. 'I'll have to wait for someone else."

"That could be a while. Tell you what, mister. We're headed down the road a couple of miles to an old store with a produce stand. There's always an old pickup parked there. I'll see if the owner can come pick you up," said the man.

"Much obliged, my friend," said Matthew.

The car drove off, and Matthew sat down to wait, removing his hat and holding it over Sara Jane's face to protect her from the sun.

Fifteen minutes later, an old, rusty pickup came rattling down the road, throwing up a dust trail behind it. A black man got out of the truck and crossed to Matthew.

"Heard ya got troubles. I'm here to help. Let's put the child and the dog in the truck bed, and you can hop in the cab with me."

Matthew and the stranger carefully lifted Sara Jane and laid her on an old blanket in the truck bed, then added Buddy, the wagon, and the gear. As they drove off down the road, the driver said, "Name's Lewis. Lewis Carter."

"Much obliged, my brother. I'm Matthew Layne. The girl's name is Sara Jane. Her dog's name is Buddy."

Lewis gave a sideways look at Matthew, surprised a white man would be so respectful of a black man.

"Where you takin' us, Lewis?" asked Matthew.

Lewis smiled and said, "I'm takin' you to my house. My wife Dolly can help you. I swear, my wife can heal anybody. Don't you worry, Matthew, my Dolly has a personal relationship with Jesus. She's got healing in her hands."

CHAPTER 45

A RELIABLE LEAD

It had been several days since the bulletins went out and notifications were sent to the railroads. There had been very little response. In fact, the only response they had had was a report from Bosque County. It turned out to be an old man with his grandson (no dog) riding a passenger train.

Sheriff Grady Black feared the girl would never be found, and he would never live it down. He didn't want to give up on the girl, but he had other cases to deal with.

There had been a shooting outside Cameron, a dispute over an inheritance. One brother was in the hospital, the other in jail. There had also been a domestic disturbance case where a drunken ex-husband was holding his ex-wife at gunpoint, upset that she had remarried.

Turns out, there was no ammo in the gun, but the man had a history of drunk and disorderly, as well as one case of assault. This latest stunt, ammo or no ammo, should keep him in prison for a good while.

Deputy Mark Hughes was out checking on a report of cattle rustling again. As the economy declined, this particular crime increased. Before that, he had gone to check out a complaint about somebody digging on somebody else's property.

It had been a busy week. Sheriff Black needed to think, so as he sat in his desk chair, he put his long, booted legs on top of his desk, tilted his Stetson over his forehead, and began wrapping twine around his left hand.

The phone rang, and the sheriff picked up on the first ring, "Sheriff Black. Uh-huh." He listened, put his legs down, and grabbed a pad and pencil. "When was this? I see. And they are sure it was her? Are these guys trustworthy? I see. I hope you told them no. Sounds like a good plan. OK, sheriff, thanks for the information and keep me posted." He hung up "Bingo," said the sheriff.

Deputy Mark Hughes walked in the door and said, "This time, it was a dozen head of cattle."

"We just got a reliable lead on the girl," said the sheriff. Sheriff Larry Gilliam from McLennan County called. Seems a couple of bulls hired by the railroad saw a notification at the train station. They said they ran off a girl with a dog and an older man who were riding in a boxcar north of Waco in McLennan County. The clincher is that the girl was pulling a small wagon. They wanted to know if there was a reward."

"If they recognized them, why didn't they detain them?" asked the deputy.

"They didn't see the notification until the followin' day."

"So, what next?" asked the deputy

"It's not in our jurisdiction, so Sheriff Gilliam is puttin' together a search party to check the area they were last seen in. It's been more than 24 hours, though, so it looks like we're a day late and a dollar short," said the sheriff.

"Oh, well. At least we know the general area she's in, which is more than we knew before." said the deputy. "By the way, you'll never guess who Festus Gibson says stole his cattle."

"Who?"

"Space aliens. Claims you can see the burned outline of their spaceship," said the deputy, laughing.

"I warned you the old coot was crazy, but this is way out even for him!" said the sheriff, joining in the laughter. "Where do ya think we should look first, Mark?"

"I was thinkin' Mars. That's where I would take my stolen cows if I was an alien," said the deputy.

"Sounds like a good place to start," said the sheriff. They both laughed as they closed the door and walked out of the office.

CHAPTER 46

SAFE HAVEN

Fifteen minutes later, they drove up in front of a small white wooden house with a screened-in porch. The house was old and in need of repair, but the yard was neat and free of debris. It could use a new roof.

"Wait here, Mr. Matthew. I'm gonna run in and tell Dolly what's goin' on."

Before he reached the porch, a large black woman came outside. She was wearing a bib apron, a cup towel in her hand. "What're you doin' home so early, Lewis? Is everything OK?"

"I'm OK," said Lewis, but I've got some folks that need our help."

They walked to the pickup, and Matthew got out.

"Mr. Matthew, this here's my wife, Dolly."

Matthew tipped his hat and said, "Nice to meet you, ma'am, My name's Matthew."

Dolly already liked this man with the nice manners and respectful attitude. "How can I help you, Mr. Matthew?"

Lewis and Matthew led Dolly to the bed of the pickup, where Sara Jane lay in a deep sleep. Buddy whined mournfully.

"Oh, my sweet Jesus! What happened to this child?" exclaimed Dolly.

"They were attacked by a large bobcat. That dog saved her life," said Matthew, realizing as he spoke that it may have been the other way around.

"Well, now, we're gonna save his life and the life of this sweet child. Lewis set up that cot on the screened-in porch. It's cooler there than inside. Mr. Matthew, as soon as the cot is set up, lay the girl on the cot, then you can bring in the dog. Lewis, once the cot is set up, put the kettle on. I need to get my medical supplies."

Because the cot had not been set up yet, Matthew brought the wagon in first, then went back for Buddy, who he carefully laid back in it. By then, the cot was set up, so with great effort, he carried in Sara Jane and laid her on it.

Matthew was concerned that Sara Jane was still asleep. She had tried so hard to be strong so Buddy could be pulled in the wagon, but she had finally succumbed to her wounds, shock, and exhaustion. She was now in a coma-like state.

"Lewis," said Dolly as she passed through the house toward the porch, "listen for the kettle whistle. When you hear it, pour some of that hot water into that big bowl and bring it in here with those old cup towels."

"Yes, Dolly," said Lewis, obeying his wife as usual.

"Mr. Matthew, bring that old milkin' stool over here, please. Then bring that foldin' chair for yourself." Dolly sat on the milking stool as Matthew unfolded the chair on the other side of Sara Jane.

"I guess I should introduce her. This here's Sara Jane. Her dog's name is Buddy."

"Well, Miss Sara Jane, Dolly and the good Lord Jesus are gonna fix you right up, don't you worry," said Dolly, carefully examining her wounds.

"Oh, this poor child. She's got some deep claw marks and one bite on her shoulder. She must have been in terrible pain," said Dolly.

"You'd never know it. She was way too busy worryin' about her dog to ever complain about her own injuries."

"That baby is in a deep sleep. The good Lord did that to help her heal," said Dolly.

The high-pitched sound of the kettle pierced the air, and Dolly called out, "Lewis, did you hear the kettle?"

"Yes, Dolly, I'm on my way," said Lewis, who wanted to say, "I'd have to be deaf not to, Dolly " but knew Dolly would frown on him sayin' that in front of a stranger.

Lewis brought in the bowl of hot water and the towels. Dolly dipped one of the small towels in the hot water, then wrung it out. She carefully wiped off the wounds, then pulled out a stone mortar and pestle. She added some herbs and honey and a small amount of water, then began to grind the herbs into a paste. She then packed Sara Jane's bite wound with the herbal paste and wrapped the wound with gauze bandage. She did the same with her claw marks.

"There now," said Dolly, "as she sleeps, that poultice will soak into her wounds and heal them."

Matthew touched Sara Jane's forehead and said, "She feels hot. Do you think she has a fever?"

"Yessir, she does, but don't worry. That's the Lord's way of gettin' all the infection out of her body. I expect it will spike in a few hours, then gradually fade. We just need to keep an eye on her during the night. I ground up some aspirin in the poultice to help with the pain."

"I am so grateful to you and Lewis, Dolly. I think you are angels in disguise," said Matthew.

Dolly laughed and said, "I been called a lot of things by white folk, Mr. Matthew, but never an angel! Truth is, if anyone is a guardian angel here, it's you and this here dog. I guess I better take a look at him."

Dolly examined his wounds and said, "Well, it don't look good. He's got even deeper claw marks then she has and at least two bites, but it ain't hopeless. We're gonna put the poultice on him like we did her, and Lord willin', we're gonna heal him. And Mr. Matthew, say a prayer that that ol' bobcat didn't have rabies."

As Dolly treated Buddy, Lewis said, "I reckon I better get back to work. Mr. James is by hisself at the store. Ya'll gonna be OK?"

"We'll be fine, Lewis. You go on. Oh, Lewis, bring some extra produce back, will ya? I need onions, potatoes, tomatoes, and greens, plus anything else that's left over at the end of the day, like usual. I want to make a big pot of soup."

"Sure thing, Dolly. Now, Mr. Matthew, go on and bring in your gear and put it on the porch. You're welcome to stay here as long as you need," said Lewis.

"Much obliged, Lewis," said Matthew.

"Mr. Matthew," said Dolly, "Why don't you lay down and rest for a bit. You gotta be worn out. I'll keep watch over her while you rest."

"Thank you, Dolly. I would like to stretch out on my bedroll for a bit. It's been a hard couple of days," said Matthew, who had started coughing.

"I'm gonna get you a glass of warm water with a little honey in it, Mr. Matthew. That will help that cough."

"Thank you."

As he lay down, Matthew realized just how exhausted and achy he was. His bad foot and leg, plus the hit he had taken on the back, were made worse by pulling the wagon and carrying the extra gear.

Dolly returned with a light blanket and a pillow for Sara Jane and handed Matthew the glass of honey water, which he gratefully sipped. "I'll leave this glass here, Mr. Matthew, so you can continue to sip on it."

"Thank you, Dolly."

Before long, Matthew fell into a much-needed sleep.

CHAPTER 47

AN OLD SOUL

When he awoke, Dolly was sitting on the old milking stool, softly singing an old gospel song.

"You sure have a mighty fine singin' voice, Dolly," said Matthew.

"Thank you kindly, Mr. Matthew. I've had nearly forty years of practice singin' in the church choir. My mother always said my sister got the looks in the family, and I got the talent. How you feelin', Mr. Matthew?"

"Much better, thank you. I guess I didn't realize just how worn out I was. How's she doin'?"

"Still sleepin', but not as deep. She was tossin' and turnin' earlier and callin' out like she was havin' a bad dream."

"She has those sometimes. That child has been through more hardship and tragedy than anyone should have to endure. Especially at such a young age," said Matthew.

"Is she your grandbaby?"

"No. She's just a little girl I met in Rockdale. Both her parents are dead, and her house burned down. Got no other family 'cept her stepfather who burned up in the fire. I'm not entirely sure how long she's been on her own."

"Oh, that poor child! And now, this. Thank God she ran into you, Mr. Matthew. You are a godsend."

"Oh, I don't know about that. I think God may have sent her to me instead of the other way around. Both she and her dog have taught me lessons in courage, faith, and unconditional love. She has given me the hope and purpose I thought I'd lost," said Matthew.

"That child is a survivor; she's an old soul," said Dolly.

"An old soul?" asked Matthew.

"Yes. An old soul is a special person chosen by God to make the world a better place. These folk have to endure more tragedy and hardship than most 'cause this makes them stronger and more compassionate. They're able to help others because they understand what other people have gone through," said Dolly.

"Sounds kinda like a sword forged in the fire to make it stronger," said Matthew.

"I like that, Mr. Matthew. A sword forged in fire. But even as strong as they are, they have to be careful. They tend to be so busy takin' care of other people that they don't take care of themselves. It can be exhaustin'."

"You sound like you speak from personal experience, Dolly," said Matthew.

Dolly smiled and said, "When my mother was on her deathbed, she told me I was an old soul. She said I had healin' in my hands. I was only eight years old at the time and didn't really understand. Later on, I discovered I had the ability to heal others with the help of Jesus Christ. I wasn't able to help everyone. I discovered that the stronger the person's faith, the easier it was to heal 'em."

"That sounds a lot like Sara Jane, except for the healin' hands. I haven't seen her do that," said Matthew.

"Not all old souls heal with their hands. Some heal with words. Sounds to me like that is more like Sara Jane," said Dolly.

"I think you're right, Dolly. She's wise beyond her years. She knows just what to say to make a person feel better." There was a long pause, then Matthew said, "How's Buddy?"

"He seems about the same but is sleepin' peacefully. I wouldn't worry too much about him. Dogs can take a lot more than people."

"Sara Jane told me that Buddy is just recoverin' from a rattlesnake bite a few weeks ago."

"Well, that's both good and bad news," said Dolly." It's bad because it means his system is probably still weak from that. The good news is that he is obviously a fighter and stronger than some. If he lived through a rattlesnake bite, then he's a survivor," said Dolly.

"Mr. Matthew, if you would like to freshen up, there's a water basin and some towels in the kitchen. The bathroom is outside, in back of the house."

"Thank you, Dolly," said Matthew, heading for the kitchen.

Just as Matthew started around the house, Lewis drove up in his pickup. He got out and called to Dolly as he walked around to the back of the pickup.

"Hey, Dolly! Come look at all this!"

He lifted a large box out of the pickup bed.

"Need some help with that, Lewis?" asked Matthew.

"Matter of fact, I could. Would you close the tailgate for me, then open the screen door?"

"Sure thing," said Matthew. When he finished helping Lewis, Matthew proceeded around to the outhouse.

Dolly signaled for Lewis to come into the kitchen so they wouldn't wake Sara Jane. "What all you got there, Lewis?"

"We hit paydirt, Dolly!" said Lewis, "I got everything you wanted, plus, when Mr. James heard about the injured girl, he threw in some ham hock and some beans."

"Oh, that's wonderful, Lewis. That'll really help build up that girl's strength. God bless Mr. James."

Lewis unloaded everything in the kitchen. As Matthew walked back, Lewis heard Matthew coughing and said, "He don't sound too good."

"I know. He's been through a lot, and he don't look too good."

"Once we get some of your good cookin' inside him and he rests up, he'll be good as new," said Lewis. "How's the girl and the dog?"

"I been prayin' and layin' on the hands. We're just gonna have to wait and see."

CHAPTER 48

WISDOM AND INTUITION

Laura was sitting in the parlor with Miss Nellie Bell, who had invited her over. They were enjoying iced tea and some of Ezelle's delicious oatmeal cookies, while Nellie Bell filled Laura in on the latest on the search for Sara Jane.

"Grady says they can't go look for her in Waco because it's not their jurisdiction. It's just so frustrating," said Nellie Bell.

"I know, and I hate feeling helpless and useless," said Laura.

"Oh, my dear. You have never been either one, "assured Nellie Bell.

"All we can do now is let the sheriff up there do his job and hope he knows what he's doing," said Laura.

"Grady assures me the sheriff there has a good reputation in law enforcement circles," said Nellie Bell.

There was a long pause, and Nellie Bell could tell that Laura was deep in thought. "Is there something else on your mind, dear?"

"I just can't stop thinking about that child. What is it about her? I've never even met her, yet I feel drawn to her," said Laura.

"I can think of a couple of reasons. First, her story is just so compelling. She's suffered so much tragedy at such a young age.

Everyone who knows her story hopes she'll be found safe. Also, you exchanged notes when she was hiding in the barn. You told me she had tried to give you money, probably all she had. You formed a kind of bond, even though you didn't know it was her."

"You always know what to say, Miss Nellie Bell. I wish I had your wisdom."

"I'll bet that when you are 94 like me, you'll be just as wise, if not more so," said Nellie Bell, laughing.

"And there's something else. I hesitate to mention it, but I don't want to burden Sam with it. Do you believe in intuition?" asked Laura.

"Well, of course, dear. All women have it, some more than others. Men have it as well, but they don't pay much attention to it ... unless they are in law enforcement like Grady, who often gets what he calls a 'gut feeling.' What is your gut telling you?"

"I'm not sure. It has something to do with my father. I haven't seen him in eight years and always assumed he was dead. But he's been on my mind lately, almost like I feel his presence."

" I understand," said Nellie Bell. "I sometimes feel Joseph's presence, especially on special days, like our anniversary. Sometimes, a smell or a sound will remind me of him, and I get goosebumps because it feels like he's here."

"So, you don't think I'm crazy?" asked Laura.

"No, dear. Of course not," said Nellie Bell.

There was a long pause, then Nellie Bell said, "Your father was Helen's favorite nephew. I think it's one of the reasons she was partial to you. You reminded her so much of him."

"I didn't know that," said Laura.

"She was devastated that he fell apart and left the family. She wanted to help him but realized that you can't help someone who doesn't want to be helped. It's a hard lesson to learn."

"I understand how she felt. I adored him. My older sister, Ellen, was closer to my mother, but I was Daddy's girl. When Ellen was in the kitchen helping Mother after supper, Daddy would read to me. My favorite book was **The Velveteen Rabbit**. He could do all the voices. I made him read it to me over and over. When I got older, we would read to each other. Our favorites were Mark Twain and Charles Dickens. It was so hard watching him slowly falling apart and not being able to help him. I was devastated when he left."

"I'm glad you have good memories to sustain you, Laura. Try to think of him as he was before, not as he was at the end," said Nellie Bell, pausing, lost in her thoughts.

"Joseph loved reading to me and I loved listening to his voice. He loved books. It's why we have such an extensive library. We even have a few leather bound first editions that Joseph cherished. His favorites were a very special Bible from Germany and **The Complete Works of William Shakespeare**, bound in leather. You are welcome to borrow any of our books," said Nellie Bell.

"Thank you," said Laura.

"'Scuse me, Miss Nellie Bell, but Odell want to know do you need anything from town. He goin' to pick up a new tire for the car," said Ezelle.

"Nothing, thank you. Oh, wait. Tell him to stop by the newspaper office and pick up a copy of this week's newspaper. I know they will deliver the paper tomorrow, but I like to get a jump on things. The paper is usually ready at 4: 00 PM," said Nellie Bell.

"Yes'm, I'll tell him."

"I really should be going, Miss Nellie Bell. I promised to make Sam fried chicken for dinner." Laura crossed to give Miss Nellie Bell a hug. "Thank you for listening to me. I always feel better after we've talked."

"You are welcome, dear. I always love seeing you. Give that sweet husband of yours a big hug from me."

CHAPTER 49

HEALING HANDS

The wonderful smell of something cooking wafted out of the kitchen and onto the screened-in porch, and Sara Jane stirred. Matthew, who had sat by her side for several hours, said, "Sara Jane, you awake, little girl?"

Sara Jane opened her eyes slightly and mumbled, "Thirsty."

"Here." He filled her cup from her canteen and helped her sit up slightly. She eagerly drank the water, then looked around and said, "Where am I?"

"You are at Lewis and Dolly Carter's house in Waco. He's the nice man who put us in his truck and brought us here. Do you remember?"

"Not really." She blinked, looked around confused, then, in a panicked voice, sat up and said, "Buddy! Where's Buddy?"

"He's OK, Sara Jane. He's right here in the wagon beside you. Dolly is nursin' you both back to health. You're safe now," said Matthew.

Pacified, Sara Jane slowly laid back down, saying, "Good. That's good." Then she fell back asleep.

Entering the porch, Dolly said, "Did I hear that child talkin'? Is she awake?"

"She roused slightly, asked for water and Buddy, then fell back asleep," said Matthew.

"That's good news, Mr. Matthew. She's makin' progress. Next time she wakes up, let me know. I'll try to feed her some of the soup. Now come on into the kitchen, and we'll have a bite."

Matthew gratefully followed Dolly into the kitchen and sat down at a small kitchen table next to Lewis. Dolly served both men a bowl of soup and some cornbread. When Dolly sat, Lewis folded his hands, and they all bowed their heads.

"Lord, we thank you for the food we are about to eat. Bless it to the nourishment of our bodies. Amen."

"This is the best meal I've had in a long time. I thank you both so much," said Matthew.

"You are most welcome, Mr. Mattthew," said Dolly.

After they had eaten, Dolly told them to go out on the porch, where it was cooler, while she cleaned up the kitchen.

Lewis brought out one of the wooden kitchen chairs, and Matthew sat in the folding chair that was already on the porch.

"Lewis," said Matthew, "you are a blessed man to have a wife like Dolly."

"I sure knows that, Mr. Matthew. She tell me that every day," said Lewis, laughing.

Matthew laughed, his laugh turning into a cough.

"You OK, Mr. Matthew?"

"Yes, thank you. I developed a cough recently. Nothin' serious. I was in Fort Worth, and it was one of those real dusty days blowin' in from the plains."

"You from Fort Worth, Mr. Matthew?"

"I'm originally from Wichita Falls but last lived in Fort Worth. I worked for the railroad but lost my job some years back."

"Man, don't I know about that. So many folk been losin' their jobs and their farms. Folks are hurtin' all over. I'm lucky I got my job with Mr. James at his store. I tend to his garden and pick the vegetables for him, then sell the produce at a stand in front of his store. He lets me take home all the produce we don't sell by the end of the day. I also do chores around the store for him, and he pays me $5 a week. ``

"That's good, Matthew. That's more than a lot of folks have these days," said Matthew.

"Dolly, she works for a white lady in town two days a week, cleanin' her house, doin 'her laundry, and cookin' for 'em. We do all right."

"Got a roof over your head, too, Lewis. You gotta lot to be thankful for," said Matthew.

"Sho do, Mr. Matthew. I thank the good Lord every day."

"I been hearin' 'bought the WPA and how they might be hirin' in Dallas. Thought I might look into it for me and a pal of mine," said Matthew.

Matthew realized that for the first time in years, he felt hope for the future. He attributed it to Sara Jane.

"Well, Mr. Matthew, I sure do wish you luck. It's gettin' dark, so I think I'll go on in. You need anything?"

"No, I'm good, Lewis. Thank you…for everything."

"'Night, Mr. Matthew."

As Lewis left, Dolly appeared in the doorway. "If you'll keep the first watch, I'll relieve you in a few hours."

"Sounds good, Dolly. Thanks so much."

During the night, Sara Jane tossed and turned from nightmares. Matthew heard her call out, "Buddy! Big cat!" and later, she mumbled something about a fire and yelled, "No, Howard! No!"

That child had been through so much. Matthew felt helpless, not being able to stop her nightmares.

Several hours later, Dolly came to relieve Matthew. "How's she doin'?

"Havin' nightmares again," said Matthew.

"Poor child. I'm gonna get her somethin' to help her sleep better."

As Dolly left the room, Sara Jane awoke. "Mr. Matthew, could I please have a drink of water?"

"Of course." Matthew poured water into her tin cup and helped her drink.

"Will you give Buddy a drink, too?"

Matthew poured water into Buddy's bowl, and the dog drank eagerly.

Dolly came back out on the porch with a cup of herbal tea and some towels. "How you feelin', Sara Jane?"

"Better. I was havin' bad dreams, but I'm better now."

Dolly felt Sara Jane's forehead and noticed her damp clothing. "Your fever broke. That's good. Mr. Matthew, will you please go into the kitchen and pour some hot water from the kettle into a large bowl and bring it here? I'm gonna check Sara Jane's wounds, then clean her up a little."

After Matthew left the room, Dolly said, "Sweet girl, we need to get you out of these wet clothes and wash you off some, OK? We're gonna cover you with these towels until I can get your clothes washed."

"I got some more clothes in my rucksack. I can wear those."

"Even better," said Dolly, who removed the pants and a shirt from the rucksack. They weren't very clean, but they would do for now.

Matthew brought a bowl filled with hot water onto the porch. "I'll go outside while you tend to Sara Jane."

Dolly helped Sara Jane out of her clothes and washed her off, then dried her. Sara winced in pain as Dolly helped her into her clothes.

"I know, sweet girl. Everything hurts. I brought you some herbal tea that will help the pain and help you sleep more peaceful."

She helped Sara Jane drink the tea and settled her back down to rest.

Dolly was checking on Buddy when Matthew returned. "She should be asleep soon. The dog is breathin' better and drank water. Animals have an amazin' ability to heal quickly. Go on and lay down now, Mr. Matthew. It's my turn to watch over her."

"Thank you, Dolly," said Matthew, coughing.

"Mr. Matthew, I'm gonna bring you some of that herbal tea and add lemon to it," said Dolly as she walked to the kitchen.

As soon as Dolly left, Sara Jane said quietly, "Mr. Matthew, is Buddy really doin' better?"

"Yes, he is. And so are you. Miss Dolly is takin' good care of both of you. She has healin' hands," said Matthew.

"Yes, she has Jesus in her hands. I can feel it. Did you hear that, Buddy, Miss Dol…" Before she finished her sentence, she was fast asleep.

Dolly returned with the tea. Matthew sipped it and started feeling better. He thanked Dolly and lay down to rest.

CHAPTER 50

SOUP AND LULLABIES

The next morning, Dolly woke up Matthew and Sara Jane. "Good mornin', Mr. Matthew. If you'll help Sara Jane sit up, I'm gonna feed her some of that soup from yesterday."

Sara Jane gratefully ate the soup and could feel a warm, peaceful feeling flow through her body. When she had eaten half the bowl, she said, "Thank you, Miss Dolly. That was so good. I feel better."

"Wonderful!" said Dolly. "We're gonna prop you up with some pillows now. I'm gonna give Buddy the rest of your soup."

Sara Jane watched as Dolly gave Buddy the soup. She was so happy to see him eating. "Mr. Matthew, would you please lift Buddy and put him on this bed with me?"

Matthew carefully lifted Buddy, who whimpered as he was laid next to Sara Jane. Sara Jane stroked Buddy's head, and Buddy licked her hand and wagged his tail.

"Buddy, Miss Dolly has healin' hands, and she's makin' us better. Don't you worry now. Before you know it, we'll be good as new."

Matthew's eyes filled with tears as Sara Jane began softly singing a lullaby to Buddy.

"Mr. Matthew," said Dolly, "come on in the kitchen. I got some breakfast for ya."

 He heard Dolly sniffling as she left the porch to return to the kitchen.

"You all right, Dolly?" asked Matthew, as he sat at the table.

Dolly was wiping her eyes with her apron. "I don't think I've ever seen anything as sweet as that child singin' lullabies to her dog. She's as hurt as he is, and all she can think about is how she can comfort him."

"She's a very special child. She makes everyone around her feel better about themselves just by bein' near her," said Matthew.

"She sho do. I hope you don't mind left-over soup for breakfast, Mr. Matthew."

"Heck no. Soups are always better the second day," said Matthew.

"Good. Then you <u>really</u> gonna love it the third day!" said Dolly, laughing.

Matthew joined in the laughter, appreciating the levity of the moment.

CHAPTER 51

MISSING COWS

Grady Black and Deputy Mark Hughes were standing in the middle of Festus Gibson's pasture.

"I come out yesterday mornin', and my cows was gone. My Jerusalem donkey, Honey, was brayin' like crazy. All that was left was this here spaceship outline. I know you don't believe me, but how else you gonna explain this?"

"I'm not sure, Festus, but there's bound to be an explanation. We'll canvas the area and ask around. Maybe someone saw somethin'," said Sheriff Black.

"Those dang aliens is dangerous! You just wait, you're gonna start hearin' about more cattle disappearin'. Maybe even people disappearin'. Hey, I bet that's what happened to that little girl that went missin'. She got sucked up into one of them spaceships. That's why you can't find her."

"I sure hope not, Festus. That's way out of our jurisdiction."

Deputy Hughes stifled a laugh.

"We'll keep you posted, Festus, and you let us know if you find anything else," said the sheriff.

As they walked back to the truck, Deputy Hughes said, "What did he mean by his 'Jerusalem' donkey?"

Sheriff Black said, "A Jerusalem donkey is a breed of donkey that has a large cross across its back. The legend is that the donkey that Jesus rode into Jerusalem on Palm Sunday was also present at his crucifixion. The donkey couldn't bear to watch Jesus crucified, so he turned away. The shadow of the cross fell on his back. God rewarded the donkey for his love of Jesus by giving him and his descendants a permanent cross across his back."

"I never heard that story before. I really like it," said the deputy.

"Mark, when we get back to the office, call Wallace Dyer and see if his twin boys are back from visitin' their grandmother in Abilene. This looks like the kind of prank they might do. I'll bet you anything they're back in Milam County."

"You may be right. I'll call Wallace. I still remember when they graduated and put a cow on top of the school roof. Did you ever figure out how they got it up there?" asked the deputy.

"Nope. It was a pain gettin' that darn thing back down, too. I wanted to arrest them for cattle rustlin', but it was their own darn cow," said the sheriff, laughing.

When they got back to the office, the phone was ringing. Sheriff Black grabbed the receiver and said, "Sheriff Black. Uh-huh. Uh-huh. How far? Oh, you did. Probably a good idea. No, nothin' here. OK, sheriff, I appreciate your efforts."

Sheriff Black hung up, a frown on his face.

"No luck?" asked the deputy.

"Nope. They searched the area in a two-mile grid. They even visited a Hooverville, five miles south of Waco, just in case they went there. Nothin'. They're in the wind. They could be anywhere," said the sheriff.

"What next? You gonna give the newspaper and Miss Nellie Bell an update?"

"I'd rather be sucked up into an alien spaceship," said the sheriff.

Deputy Hughes laughed, and the sheriff joined in.

CHAPTER 52

HARD LIFE LESSONS

Two more days passed and both Sara Jane and Buddy were recovering nicely under Dolly's tender care. Their wounds were still painful, but there was no more inflammation.

Matthew was feeling stronger, as well, although he couldn't get rid of his cough. Dolly's lemon and honey mixture helped soothe it, however. Now that Sara Jane was on the mend, Matthew started accompanying Lewis to work.

He enjoyed helping Lewis pick the vegetables and set up the produce stand. It made Lewis's day easier and gave him a sense of accomplishment. Lewis appreciated the help and enjoyed Matthew's company.

When Mr. James discovered that Matthew was good with a hammer, he put him to work around the store. Matthew repaired shelves and steps and expanded the produce stand. Matthew even made suggestions about rearranging the inside of the store.

Business improved significantly, and Matthew was rewarded with a ten-dollar bonus, the first money he had received since starting there two weeks ago. Matthew insisted upon giving Lewis and Dolly the money "for my room and board", but Lewis only accepted half of it, telling Matthew to keep the rest. "Besides," said Lewis, "you been doin' half my work for two weeks and wouldn't take no money."

Three days later, after everyone had gone to sleep, they were awakened by Buddy barking. "Quiet, Buddy!" said Sara Jane. When Buddy continued to bark, Sara Jane knew something was wrong. Matthew woke up and was joined by the Carters.

"I smell smoke," said Dolly.

"Me, too," said Sara Jane.

The two men, lacking the females' olfactory senses, didn't smell anything but agreed to look around. When they walked outside, the wind shifted, and there was definitely the smell of smoke in the air.

Suddenly, a neighbor came running by, shouting, "It's the school! The school's on fire!"

People started gathering, and Lewis said, "OK, everybody, get a bucket and head to the school. We'll set up a bucket brigade." The neighbors complied, and after grabbing buckets, they ran to the school, lining up at the water pump.

The buckets of water helped extinguish the fire and kept it from spreading. Fortunately, they had gotten there early enough to keep the school from completely burning down.

Dolly noticed something burning in the grass in front of the school, and her anger bubbled over. A large cross was burning in the grass. Dolly called out to Lewis, who ran over to her. She pointed out the cross, and she, Lewis, and Matthew put out the burning cross.

Most of the fire had been extinguished, but the partially collapsed building continued to smolder. "This weren't no accident," said Lewis.

"I'm afraid not, Lewis. This was a deliberate act of hate," said Matthew.

"But who would do such a thing?" asked Sara Jane.

Matthew took Sara Jane's hand and said, "Let's go home, Sara Jane. We need to clean up a little, and Dolly and Lewis need to talk with their neighbors."

When they returned home, they washed off in the kitchen basin. Matthew put on a pot of coffee, then he and Sara Jane sat at the small kitchen table. Matthew was silent for a couple of minutes, trying to gather his thoughts and decide how to explain things to Sara Jane. He rose and poured himself a cup of coffee, offering Sara Jane a cup of milk.

Matthew sat back down, took a slow sip of his coffee, then, with his hands still holding the cup, he finally spoke. "Sara Jane, I know you noticed the cross burnin' in the grass in front of the school. That cross is evidence that a group of bad white folk called the Ku Klux Klan are responsible for settin' the school on fire. These people have hate in their hearts for people who don't look like them. They wear white hoods and robes to disguise their appearance. They are cowards and don't want anyone to know who they are. I'm sorry you had to see that, but you need to know about them because they exist, and we need to be aware of them," said Matthew.

"But why do they hate colored people so much? It don't make sense to me," said Sara Jane.

"That's because you were raised right, Sara Jane. You were taught that we are all God's children, and everyone should be treated the same. These people weren't born this way. They were taught hate by adults. I think these people have hate in their hearts because they feel so miserable about themselves that they think they need to bully and attack people they feel are beneath them. This gives them a sense of power," said Matthew.

"Oh, I just hate that they do that!" said Sara Jane.

When Dolly and Lewis entered the kitchen, Matthew said, "I hope it's OK. I put on a pot of coffee."

"Oh, good," said Dolly, sitting down, a troubled look on her face. Lewis brought Dolly and himself a cup of coffee and joined them at the table. They were all quiet for a couple of minutes, then Sara Jane spoke.

"I'm so sorry about the fire. Mr. Matthew told me about the bad white people who did that. I just hate them!"

"No, baby, don't hate them, or you become like them, and there's already too much hate floatin' around," said Dolly.

"I'm sorry, Miss Dolly. You're right. I remember Mama tellin' me that Jesus always loves us, but he hates the bad things we do. I guess I'll hate what they do, but I'll try not to hate them. I bet Jesus is just shakin' his head," said Sara Jane.

"That's right, baby. Jesus is surely shakin' his head." Dolly rose from the table and continued, "Well, it's gettin' late. Lewis and me need to clean up a little, then let's all go back to bed and get a few more hours sleep before mornin'."

No one slept that night…not even Buddy.

CHAPTER 53

SOUL WEARY

It had been three days since the fire. Matthew continued helping Lewis and the neighbors clean up the rubble from the burned school. Some of it had been destroyed, but part of it was OK, except for the pervasive smell of smoke. Fortunately, school was out for the summer. They would have time to rebuild what they could before fall.

Matthew was soul weary. His body ached from helping Lewis at the school and at work. He was also preoccupied with something he knew he had to do.

That night, after Sara Jane had gone to bed, Matthew met with Dolly and Lewis in the kitchen. "Lewis, Dolly, you've been a real blessing to me and Sara Jane. You've been like the family we both lost. But there's one more thing I need to ask of you. I need to go to Milam County and look for my daughter. I want to find her and ask her forgiveness. It's somethin' I need to do alone. Would it be OK if I leave Sara, Jane and Buddy here while I do that? It should only take a few days."

"Mr. Matthew," said Dolly, "that child can stay here the rest of her life if she wants to. I love her like my own. You just go do what you need to do, and we'll all be here when you get back."

"When are you plannin' on leavin'?" asked Lewis.

"I thought I'd leave this comin' Sunday. That'll give me a few more days to help at the store. Mr. James promised me three more dollars, and that's enough to buy new shoes. That and the five dollars he gave me before will be enough to buy a new shirt and pants. I need to clean myself up and talk to Sara Jane about all this, so please don't say anything yet. Lewis, do you think you could cut my hair and help me trim my beard?"

"Glad to help," said Lewis.

The next day, after Lewis and Matthew got home from shopping, Matthew suggested that he, Sara Jane, and Buddy take a walk. As they walked, Matthew explained his plan to Sara Jane.

"Will you be OK with that, Sara Jane?"

"Are you sure Buddy and I can't go with you, Mr. Matthew?"

"Not this time, Sara Jane. This is somethin' I need to do by myself."

"OK, Mr. Matthew, but Buddy and me sure will miss you. I'm real proud of you for decidin' to go find her. How long you gonna be gone?"

"Well, I'm plannin' to hitchhike and walk when I have to. I reckon it'll take me a couple of days to get to Rockdale, then I'll need to pay a visit to someone who might know whether or not she's there. If she isn't there, I'll head on back, but if she's there, I'll be another day or so."

"OK, Mr. Matthew. Buddy and I will wait for you here. I'll pray you have a safe trip and your daughter welcomes you. She'll be mighty lucky to have you."

"Thank you, Sara Jane."

Despite her brave front, Sara Jane did not like the idea of Matthew traveling alone. What if something happened to him, and she and Buddy weren't there to help him? Nor did she like the idea of staying with the Carters by herself. She had grown to love Dolly and Lewis, but it would not be the same without Matthew. What if something happened to prevent him from coming back for her?

CHAPTER 54

SPRINGTIME STORMS

Early Sunday morning, Matthew prepared to leave. He gathered up his bedroll, and, at her insistence, Sara Jane's rucksack containing her canteen. He folded his new clothes and placed them in the rucksack and grabbed Sara Jane's walking stick. Dolly had packed Matthew a sandwich, which he added to the rucksack.

"Now, Mr. Matthew, you be real careful. We all gonna pray that you have a safe trip. Don't you worry about anything here. You take as long as you need," said Dolly.

"Thank you, Dolly."

Lewis walked Matthew to his pickup truck. He offered to drive Matthew to the crossroads heading out of town to give him a head start on his trip. Matthew was grateful, as it would save him ten miles of walking.

To his amazement, as he was getting in the truck, Sara Jane, followed by Buddy, ran to him, threw her arms around his neck and said," I love you, Mr. Matthew. Promise to come back for me!"

Matthew climbed into the truck, tears blurring his eyes. "I promise, Sara Jane."

When they arrived at the crossroads, Lewis said, "Mr. Matthew, we'll take real good care of that sweet girl. You just concentrate on findin' your daughter. Take care, now."

"Thank you, Lewis." Matthew climbed out of the truck, gathered his gear, and headed down the road. Matthew was grateful the temperature was mild that day, and the skies were cloudy. Texas weather was unpredictable and could change in a heartbeat. A late spring day could be cool or oppressively hot, sometimes on the same day. He had been able to catch a ride earlier, but the driver was a farmer whose property was five miles down the way. Still, five miles riding was better than five miles walking.

Spring is beautiful in Texas, but it's no paradise. Matthew knew that lurking behind every bluebonnet and Indian paintbrush wildflower was the possibility of thunderstorms, hailstorms, and tornadoes. And yes, Texas has an occasional hurricane in its coastal areas, but hurricanes give plenty of warning, while tornadoes can develop in a matter of hours and strike in a matter of minutes.

Matthew had experienced several tornadoes firsthand in Wichita Falls and Fort Worth. He knew that the Waco area had experienced some destructive tornadoes in the past, and he knew the signs to look for.

Despite an uneasy feeling, Matthew felt compelled to leave for Milam County that day. He told himself that if he waited for everything to be perfect, he'd never make the trip. He had walked for over an hour without anyone stopping to give him a ride. He was grateful to have Sara Jane's walking stick, as his bad foot and leg were already hurting.

The skies darkened, and it started to rain, then hail. Matthew covered his head with his bedroll and looked around for shelter. Just as the hail fell harder, he spotted an old, abandoned farmhouse. As he looked up, he saw a huge column cloud and noticed the air had become still, and the sky was grayish green in color.

Matthew took off running, no easy task for an older man with a bad leg and foot. He knew a tornado was forming and that he would have only a matter of minutes if a funnel cloud appeared. Just as he reached the old farmhouse, he heard what he never hoped to hear again: the roar of a train that was not really a train, coming his way. He could see that three funnels were dipping down from the clouds, two small ones and one large one that was much closer, and the source of the train-like roar.

Matthew had to find cover now. He knew houses in Texas did not typically have basements, but most farmhouses had root cellars. He ran to the back of the house, located the root cellar, opened its door, and dashed down the cellar steps. He tripped on the last step and fell forward onto the bottom of the cellar. He placed the bedroll over his head for additional protection. He could hear debris flying everywhere as the funnel hit the area around the house. The roar became louder as boards were splintered and windows exploded. He could hear the roof being ripped off the house.

By the time Matthew had finished praying, the tornado had moved on. It had only lasted a matter of minutes, but those minutes had been intense. He was grateful to be alive, but would he be able to get out of the cellar, or would the door be piled with heavy debris, trapping him?

He climbed up the cellar steps, his bad foot hurting even more from twisting it in the fall. The cellar door was heavy, too heavy. Matthew prayed, "Lord, you've taken me this far. I ask your help in gettin' this door open. I can't do this alone." Whether it was divine intervention or Matthew's determination, he pushed and pushed until he was able to get the door partially open, the heaviest debris falling to the side. He then reached around the door and managed to push away some additional debris until he was able to get the door completely open.

When he climbed out of the cellar, Matthew looked around at the destruction. The house was completely destroyed. Debris was everywhere, including an old rusty plow embedded in an uprooted tree. Matthew's heart pounded as he realized he could have easily been killed. He gave a prayer of thanks for his deliverance. He checked the sky and didn't see any additional funnel clouds. They had either changed direction or been sucked back up into the sky.

Matthew decided to go back into the cellar and wait a while longer in case another funnel formed. As he sat on one of the steps, a terrible thought occurred to him: Did one of those tornadoes hit the Carter's house? Were they or Sara Jane injured? Oh, dear God! Please let them be OK.

CHAPTER 55

SOMETIMES THE SKIES ARE CLOUDY

That Sunday morning, after Matthew left, the Carters and Sara Jane got ready for church. This was the first time they had taken Sara Jane with them, and Dolly had made sure Sara Jane would look nice. She had taken one of her old "skinny" dresses she knew she would never be able to fit into again and made it into a dress for Sara Jane. There was no money for new shoes, but Dolly made sure Sara Jane's old lace-up shoes were cleaned and polished. She put thick cardboard in the soles so the holes wouldn't show.

As they walked to church, Dolly looked at the sky and said, "Looks like it's gonna come a cloud."

"Sho do," said Lewis, "Hope it don't rain 'til we get home from church."

When they reached the church, Sara Jane reminded Buddy to wait on the porch. As they entered the church, they were greeted by the pastor. As he shook the preacher's hand, Lewis introduced Sara Jane and said, "Preacher, hope you don't mind, but this little girl's dog is used to waitin' on the church porch durin' the service."

"Glad to have him here," said the preacher, "he ain't a Catholic, is he?"

Lewis and the preacher laughed, then Sara Jane said, "No sir, Buddy's a Methodist." The preacher laughed again, but Sara Jane was totally serious.

Several members of the congregation greeted them as they sat in their usual pew. Dolly usually sang in the choir but wanted to sit next to Sara Jane her first time here. Dolly handed Sara Jane a colorful cardboard fan decorated with an advertisement for the local funeral parlor. Sara Jane noticed several ladies fanning themselves, so she did the same.

As she looked around, Sara Jane noticed how colorfully the ladies were dressed. Every lady was wearing a large hat. Most of the ladies in her church back home wore hats, but they were smaller and less colorful. Sara Jane decided that when she was grown, she would have a big blue hat with feathers and seashells.

Sara Jane enjoyed the service. It was longer than she was used to, but the preacher spoke with such passion, and the singing was so enthusiastic that she hated for it to end. She and Dolly continued singing on the way home.

The sky was much cloudier, and just as they arrived home, it started to hail. As they ran into the house, Lewis said, "Well, we dodged that bullet!"

They changed out of their church clothes, and Dolly and Sara Jane started to fix lunch. As she looked out the kitchen window, Dolly noticed how still the air had become. The sky was turning a grayish green. Dolly ran through the house, looked up and saw three funnel clouds in the distance. "Lewis!" called Dolly, "there's three funnel clouds formin'. One of 'ems bigger and closer. Better get Sara Jane and Buddy in the closet."

Just as Lewis got Sara Jane and Buddy in the closet, they heard a loud roar like a train coming. They knew what that meant. They each grabbed a pillow and slid under the bed. They heard the screen being ripped off the screened-in porch. The tornado touched the ground, sending debris everywhere, bursting windows, and breaking wood. Buddy barked wildly. The house shook. Then, as quickly as the tornado had touched down, it switched directions and moved away from the house. The house was quiet.

Lewis crawled out from under the bed and yelled for Dolly and Sara Jane to stay in place. He ran outside and checked the sky. He saw only one small funnel in the distance that seemed to be traveling in the opposite direction. The color of the sky was returning to normal. Lewis returned and told Dolly and Sara Jane it was safe to come out.

"You OK, sweet girl?" asked Dolly.

"Yes, ma'am. Are y'all OK?"

They joined Lewis, who was checking out the damage. Two windows were broken, the screen ripped off the porch, and a corner of the bedroom roof was torn off. Lewis's truck was on its side but otherwise looked OK. They walked around the back and saw that the outhouse was remarkably untouched.

"Well," said Lewis, " it could have been a lot worse. We have a lot to be thankful for."

"Yes, we do," said Dolly.

Suddenly, Sara Jane said, "Oh, no! Mr. Matthew is walkin' down the road. What if the tornado heads his way?" She fell to her knees and prayed for Matthew's safety.

CHAPTER 56

KEEP MOVING FORWARD

Matthew continued to rest in the cellar. His foot and leg were aching, and his arms and back were sore from pushing open the cellar door. He would not be able to check on Sara Jane and the Carter's until much later. Neither he nor they had a telephone. All he could do was trust in God that they were unharmed and keep moving forward.

Matthew made the decision to spend the night in the cellar. The weather was still unstable, and he couldn't risk being on the road should it start to hail or form another funnel cloud. He ate half of the sandwich Dolly had given him and drank from Sara Jane's canteen. He suddenly felt very lonely. These past several weeks, he had grown used to traveling with Sara Jane and Buddy. It wasn't the same without them. Had he done the right thing leaving them with the Carter's?

Once again, he prayed for their safety, then he lay down on his bedroll and slept.

When morning came, Matthew arose and checked the weather. The sun was shining as though the tornado had never happened, but the destruction surrounding him confirmed that there had, indeed, been a bad tornado. Matthew ate a few bites of the sandwich, then grabbed his gear and climbed out of the cellar. He was sore and achy all over, and his cough had worsened, but he needed to get back on the road.

Matthew walked back toward the main road, hoping he could catch a ride with someone. He began painfully walking but stopped and put out his thumb when he heard a vehicle coming. Thankfully, the pickup stopped, and the driver offered him a ride.

"I'm headin' to Cameron," said the driver, "will that work for ya?"

"Perfect," said Matthew as he painfully climbed into the pickup. Cameron was in the right direction, although it was still fifteen miles from Rockdale. One step at a time, thought Matthew, one step at a time. Matthew noticed the man had come from the direction of Waco. "Do you know if the tornado hit Waco yesterday?"

"Sure did," said the driver. "I spent the afternoon in my storm cellar with my family. I was supposed to drive to Cameron yesterday, but the storm kept me home."

"What part of Waco did it hit?" asked Matthew.

"All over. There were three separate funnels spotted. They kind of took off in different directions. I listened to the radio last night. Apparently, the funnels did damage, but no deaths have been reported. The funnels were not as wide as some have been in the past, so some areas of Waco were untouched. One fella swears his cows was picked up and set down in a neighborin' pasture, and another man reported his pickup truck disappeared. I reckon it'll show up somewhere."

Matthew was concerned that the tornadoes had hit Waco as he had feared, but he was grateful no deaths had been reported.

"You weren't out walkin' yesterday, were ya?" asked the driver.

"Yep. took off runnin' and found shelter in a root cellar."

"I thought ya looked a little banged up," said the driver.

"I'll take banged up over dead any day," said Matthew.

"Good point," said the driver. "Well, mister. I'm gonna let you out at this here fillin' station. I have to drive to a place out in the country outside Cameron."

"Much obliged," said Matthew as he climbed out of the pickup.

Matthew bought a cold drink from the store, ensuring that he could use their bathroom. It felt good to wash up and change into his new clothes. They were wrinkled but clean. With any luck, he would be able to catch another ride from someone heading to Rockdale.

CHAPTER 57

SWEET REUNION

Luck was with Matthew. He approached a driver who was filling up his car and asked where the man was heading. The man told him he was going to Caldwell, and Matthew was welcome to come along.

"Much obliged," said Matthew, "I'm goin' to Rockdale, so if you don't mind droppin' me at the crossroads in Milano, that'll help a lot."

"Hop in," said the driver. "You got family in Rockdale?"

"No, but I got friends there who might help me locate some of my family in Milam County."

"That's good. Family is important…especially these days. We all need the support to get us through hard times. My family is in Caldwell. I got a wife and five kids. We run the mercantile in Caldwell, and all but my youngest help out."

"You are a blessed man," said Matthew.

"I thank the good Lord every day. I know people are sufferin' out there. Lots of folks don't have a home or enough food to eat. My wife and I do what we can to help out."

"We all need to do that. It would sure be a better world if we did," said Matthew.

The driver slowed down, then stopped at the side of the road.

"Here's the crossroads. Is this spot OK?" asked the driver.

"Perfect," said Matthew. "Much obliged. God bless you and your family."

"Thank you, my friend. Good luck findin' your family."

Matthew climbed out of the car and started down the road toward Milano, which was about eight miles from Rockdale. He had walked about two miles when he put out his thumb and flagged down a pickup truck. He had intended to walk further, but his injured foot, bad leg, and achy body slowed him down. His chest was hurting, and his cough had grown worse.

The pickup driver was going to Taylor and had to pass through Rockdale to get there, so he kindly offered Matthew a ride. He dropped Matthew in town, only one block from Miss Nellie Bell's house.

When Matthew arrived at the huge house, he stopped at the end of the sidewalk, memories from his childhood and young adult visits passing through his mind. Whenever he had visited Aunt Helen, she had brought him here to visit with her best friend, Nellie Bell. His Aunt Helen had doted on him, and Miss Nellie Bell always treated him like her own. She had tried to interest him in the piano, but he preferred sliding down the huge stair banister and exploring the house, pretending it was a huge fort built to protect them from the Indians. Matthew said a silent prayer that she was still alive and well.

Matthew approached the front door, dropping his gear on the porch. A thin black woman answered his knock. What was her name? Esther? Anna? He couldn't remember her name. It had been too long. Was it the same woman?

"Yes, can I help you, sir?"

"I hope so. I'm lookin' for Nellie Bell Richards. Does she still live here?"

"Yessir, she do. May I tell her who's callin' on her?"

"Tell her it's her friend Helen's nephew, Matthew. Matthew Layne."

"Mr. Matthew? I didn't recognize you. Come on in. Do you remember me? I'm Ezelle. Stay here just a minute and let me tell her you're here. She gonna be so happy to see you."

"Thank you, Ezelle," said Matthew.

Ezelle returned a moment later and led Matthew into the parlor, where Miss Nellie Bell reclined on her chaise lounge. She looked so tiny, like she had shrunk.

"Matthew! As I live and breathe! Come give me a hug!" exclaimed Nellie Bell.

Removing his hat, Matthew hugged her and noticed she had tears in her eyes. He had no idea he meant so much to her.

"Oh, if only Helen were still alive to see you!"

"So, she passed?" said Matthew.

"About a year and a half ago. I miss her every day. Have a seat, Matthew. Ezelle, will you bring us some iced tea, please?"

"Yes'm."

"Matthew, I'm so happy to see you, but I must say, you don't look well," said Nellie Bell.

"I'm just feelin' a little under the weather. Just a bit tired," said Matthew, coughing.

"Matthew, I don't mean to pry, but where have you been all these years? We thought you were dead."

"It's a long story, Miss Nellie Bell, and one I'm not too proud of. When I left my family eight years ago, I was a broken man. I spent seven of those years ridin' the rails, just tryin' to ease my pain with alcohol. About a year ago, a preacher in one of those tent revivals led me to Jesus. I cleaned up my act and swore to be a better man. I wanted to find my family and make amends, but I was ashamed and lacked the courage. Then I met someone who taught me about courage and forgiveness. This friend encouraged me to find my family. That's why I'm here." Matthew paused to take a drink of his tea, then continued. "I looked for them in Ft. Worth and discovered that Emily and Ellen had gone to Oklahoma, then California. I was told Laura and her husband had moved to Dallas, then later to Milam County after they inherited some property. Was it Aunt Helen's property?"

"Yes, it was, Matthew. Laura and her husband moved into Helen's farmhouse a few months after she passed away," said Nellie Bell. 'Matthew, forgive me, but you aren't running from the law, are you?"

Matthew laughed, "No, ma'am. The worst I've done is ride the freight trains. I know that's illegal, but I figure the sheriff's got bigger fish to fry."

"Good. I'm just trying to protect Laura. So, all you want to do is ask her forgiveness?"

"That's all. It weighs heavy on my heart. I won't rest 'til I see her ."

"Then what, Matthew?"

"I don't know for sure. Depends on how it goes. If she'll see me, I'll ask her forgiveness, then get on with my life and let her get on with hers. I'm hopin' to find work somewhere. Maybe Dallas."

There was a long pause, then Matthew said," Miss Nellie Bell, truth is, I don't know if she'll want to see me or not. I don't want to just drop in and surprise her."

"Matthew, I can assure you that she will want to see you. She was just here a few days ago, talking about how much she missed you. How about this? I will call her at the farm, tell her you are here, and ask if she would be willing to see you," said Nellie Bell.

"I would appreciate that so much."

"But Matthew, first things first. You look famished and exhausted. Let's have lunch and a short rest, OK?"

"Thank you. That's a great idea," said Mattthew.

CHAPTER 58

CRAZY MARY

Sheriff Grady Black was outside his office getting a file out of his truck when the phone rang inside his office. Deputy Mark Hughes picked up the receiver. "Deputy Hughes."

"Deputy Hughes, this is John Maines, Chief of Police in Rockdale. Is the boss in?"

Deputy Hughes smiled. He got a kick out of the fact that John Maines, a man he'd known for thirty years, felt the need to introduce himself so formally. "Hold on, John. He's comin' in the door." The deputy laid the receiver on its side and walked to the door to give the sheriff a heads-up. "You're not gonna believe who's on the line: 'Chief of Police' John Maines," said the deputy, with a smirk.

"What the heck does he want?" asked the sheriff.

"He didn't say. He just asked for you," said the sheriff.

Sheriff Black picked up the receiver. "Jim, Grady here. To what do I owe the pleasure?"

"Same ol' smart aleck, I see. Any leads on the missing girl?" asked the chief.

"Nope. How 'bout you? You hear any talk?"

"Matter of fact, I might have a lead for ya. I got a call yesterday from a fella in Waco. He saw the bulletin at the Waco railroad station and says he might know where the girl is. Says he works part-time at a grocery and produce stand in north Waco, and he overheard another worker and his boss talkin' 'bout a white girl and an older fella stayin' with him and his wife," said the chief.

Sheriff Grady suddenly sat up with interest and grabbed a pencil. "You got the fella's name and phone number?"

"I asked him for his info, and all he said was, 'Is there a reward?' when I told him 'No', he hung up," said the chief.

"A real model citizen," said the sheriff, disappointed. "Well, thanks for lettin' me know. Ya never know what a clue can lead to."

"You're welcome. And, uh, Grady, there's somethin' else," said the chief.

Grady was waiting for the other shoe to drop. It wasn't like John to offer information unless he wanted something in exchange.

"How can I help you, John?" asked the sheriff.

"Two words: Crazy Mary."

"Crazy Mary?" asked the sheriff.

Crazy Mary was a skinny, middle-age black woman who scooted around downtown Rockdale by propelling herself on a square board with wheels. This alone was odd enough, but she muttered to herself as she shook her head from side to side and made sputtering sounds with her lips. She loved to grab the telephone poles and swing around them. People found her odd, but entertaining.

"What about her?" asked the sheriff.

"Well," said the chief, "she's become a real menace. She's added some new things to her repertoire. Now she curses and spits at people and makes chicken and other animal noises."

"Is she any good?" asked the sheriff, secretly smiling.

"What do you mean?" asked the chief.

"At the animal noises. Is she any good?" asked the sheriff.

"You're makin' light of this, Grady, but it's become a real problem. Yesterday, she got to spinnin' around that telephone pole so fast she slung herself out into traffic, still on the board, and caused a wreck. And Grady, it was Mayor George Yoakum's car and his grandson Bobby's pickup. Something's got to be done."

"I agree, John, but why are you callin' me about this? You're the Chief of Police in Rockdale. That's your jurisdiction, not mine."

"I'm aware of that, Grady, but her daddy refuses to talk to me. Says he'll only talk to Sheriff Grady because y'all have history."

"Well, he's right about that. I've had to visit the old man several times over the years. One time it was for a moonshine still in his backyard that was smokin' like a chimney and caught his outhouse on fire. Another time, he climbed up on the neighbor's roof, refusin' to come down until they gave him their dog," said the sheriff.

"Did they give it to him?" asked the chief.

"Nope. They didn't have a dog. I got him to come down by offerin' him some beef jerky," said the sheriff. "The last time I went out there was because some property owners filed a complaint against him for puttin' up 'No Trespassing' signs."

"What's wrong with that?" asked the chief.

"It wasn't his property," said the sheriff.

"Oh, my Lord," said the chief, "the whole darn family must be crazy."

"Pretty much," said the sheriff.

"So, will you talk to the old man?" asked the chief.

"OK, I'll give it a try. But you're gonna owe me," said the sheriff, hanging up and sighly deeply. He related the story of Crazy Mary's latest antics to Deputy Hughes. They both laughed heartily at the thought of her spinning herself into the street while clucking like a chicken.

"Sorry I missed that," said the deputy.

Later that day, the sheriff was on his way home from his visit with Crazy Mary's daddy. Her daddy said he couldn't leave her at home when he came to town because she got into the moonshine (which, by the way, he no longer made, or so he claimed). The sheriff struck a deal with him: when he came to Rockdale, he was to check in with the Chief of Police's office, and either the chief or his deputy would supervise her. He couldn't wait to tell the chief. He smiled at the prospect.

On his way home, the sheriff swung by the Sandy Creek Methodist Church. He had gotten in the habit of doing this since the search for the little girl had begun. He thought maybe she might have circled back and sought refuge somewhere in the church.

After checking the church, he decided to take a walk in the church cemetery, where the bluebonnets still bloomed beautifully. How could you not love the state flower of Texas? He soon came to the gravesites he was searching for: James Evans, Mary Evans, Baby Boy Mills. "Baby Boy Mills? How curious," he said. Then he noticed "Little Jimmy" scratched on the back of the wooden cross.

He figured the little girl had wanted the baby to have a name. She had named him after her father rather than her stepfather, whose baby it was. That said a lot about how she felt about her stepfather.

And speaking of Howard Mills, why wasn't he buried here next to his wife and baby? He would ask the coroner when he got back to Cameron. As he stood there pondering the situation, someone called out his name.

"Sheriff Black?" called the woman.

The sheriff turned and saw Laura Patterson walking toward him, a bunch of wildflowers in her arms.

"Hello, Mrs. Patterson, good to see you," said the sheriff.

"Nice to see you, too, sheriff. Please call me Laura. Do you have family buried here?"

"No. My family are all buried in Rockdale. I was just checkin' out the graves of Sara Jane Evans' family. Just curious, really," said the sheriff.

"I can't imagine how terrible it was for her to lose both parents at such a young age, then have to live with a neglectful, bitter stepfather. On top of that, her house burns down, leaving her with nobody and no place to go," said Laura.

"Yep, it's a real tragedy. What brings you here, Laura?" asked the sheriff.

"My Great-Aunt Helen is buried here. We also buried our baby girl here last fall. Her name is Emily, after my mother," said Laura. "I place flowers on their graves once a month."

"I'm so sorry, Laura. I had no idea about your baby."

"When I found out the missing girl's family was also buried here, I started placing flowers on their graves, as well. It's another bond I share with her," said Laura, "makes me feel like I'm doing something for her."

"I'm sure she would appreciate that. I couldn't help noticin' that her stepfather isn't buried here. Any idea why?" asked the sheriff.

"Miss Nellie Bell told me he was buried in Rockdale next to his mother and father. They have a family plot there."

"I see. That makes sense," said the sheriff, wondering if there was anything Nellie Bell didn't know about.

"I guess there's no news about Sara Jane's disappearance?" asked Laura.

"Not really. Mostly rumors and talk, but nothin' concrete," said the sheriff. "I'm not givin' up, though. We'll find her eventually." The sheriff hoped it wasn't just wishful thinking.

"Nice seeing you, sheriff. If you can wait just a minute while I lay these flowers on their graves, I'll walk out with you."

"I'd like that," said the sheriff.

As he drove home, the sheriff was thinking of Laura Patterson. What a sweet woman she was! And she was easy on the eyes, too. Hold on. Better not go down that path. She was a married woman. He was thirty-seven years old; why hadn't he found a woman like that? As soon as he had that thought, he could hear Nellie Belle saying, "Now Matthew, I've introduced you to several lovely ladies over the years. You won't give them a chance." She was right about that. Nellie Bell's idea of "lovely" and Matthews' idea of "lovely" were two different things. Except when it came to Laura Patterson.

CHAPTER 59

THE PRODIGAL FATHER

Two hours later, Ezelle brought Nellie Bell the phone. Nervous and wanting to give Nellie Bell privacy, Matthew walked out to the large front porch.

"Ezelle, do you remember Laura's number?" asked Nellie Bell.

"It's the same as Miss Helen's, Miss Nellie Bell."

"Oh, silly me! Of course. I guess I'm just nervous," said Nellie Bell as she dialed the number.

After three rings, Laura picked up. "Hello?"

"Laura? It's Nellie Bell. I have a wonderful surprise for you, but I need to see if you are willing to accept it."

"A surprise? I don't understand."

"Laura, are you willing to see your father?"

"My father? He's alive? Where is he?" said Laura.

"He's here, Laura, pacing back and forth on my front porch. He wants to see you, but he's afraid you won't want to see him."

"This is so…so incredible! Of course I'll see him. Should I come there?"

"No, he wants to come to you. I'll have Odell drive him. And Laura dear, be prepared for his appearance. He's lost a lot of weight and has aged quite a bit. He doesn't look well. He should be there in about thirty minutes, OK?"

"OK, and thank you, Miss Nellie Bell. This is so wonderful!" She hung up.

"Ezelle, will you tell Matthew to come in now, please."

"Yes'm."

When Matthew entered the parlor, he was shaking.

"Matthew, Laura has agreed to see you. In fact, she seemed quite delighted at the prospect. I'll have Odell drive you, dear. Ezelle, will you please have Odell bring the car around?"

"Already told 'em. He's on the way," said Ezelle with a smile.

"I'm mighty grateful, Miss Nellie Bell. This means so much to me," said Matthew.

" You are very welcome, Matthew. I'm happy to help. There's Odell with the car. Now, Mathhew, she may need a little time, dear. I'm sure this is quite a shock."

"Of course," said Matthew, gathering up his gear.

"Just leave all that here, Matthew. Ezelle will put it in a room for you. You can get it when you get back. And Matthew, no matter what happens, you'll always be welcome here. Best of luck."

"Thank you."

As he climbed in the front passenger seat, Matthew introduced himself to Odell, who remembered him as a boy.

"Wouldn't you rather sit in the back, Mr. Matthew?"

"No, Odelle, I'd rather sit up here with you if it's OK with you."

"Yessir, not a problem." Odell smiled and appreciated that this white man treated him as an equal.

As they drove up to the farmhouse, Matthew's palms started to sweat. In fact, he was sweating all over and coughing more. He hesitated to get out but saw his daughter walk out onto the front porch.

"Would you like me to stay awhile, Mr. Matthew?" asked Odell.

"That's a good idea. I might be headin' back in a few minutes."

Matthew climbed out of the car, and Odell moved the car under a shade tree. He slowly walked toward the porch, his heart pounding, but before he could reach it, Laura ran down the steps and embraced her father.

"Oh, Daddy! Where have you been? I thought you were dead. I've missed you so much!"

Matthew started sobbing, and his whole body shook. He never dreamed she would welcome him in this way.

"Come on the porch and sit down, Daddy. I made lemonade the way you always liked it, with lots of sugar."

As Laura led Matthew to one of the rockers, he removed his hat and pulled out his handkerchief and dabbed at his eyes and nose. Laura, her eyes filled with tears, poured both of them a glass of lemonade.

"Daddy, how on earth did you find me?"

"I went to our old house in Fort Worth., hoping you were all still there. A neighbor told me your mother and sister were in Oklahoma first, then traveled to California. She mentioned that you and your husband moved to Milam County because y'all had inherited some property there. I remembered that Aunt Helen had a place here and put two and two together. Miss Nellie Bell confirmed my hunch."

"I'm so happy you found me, Daddy. I've really missed you!"

"Oh, Laura," said Matthew, "I am so sorry for all the pain I have caused you. When I left, I was a broken man. I was both physically and spiritually injured. I lost my job and lost my wife to my boss. I don't know if you can understand what that does to a man. I know that's no excuse for what I done, but I'm just tryin' to explain why I left."

Laura knelt at her father's feet. "Oh, Daddy, we are all broken in some way. We all have cracks. But Jesus loves a challenge. He loves putting all our pieces back together for us."

"I just want you to know that I always loved you and am heartily sorry for my actions. I'm a different man now, Laura. I accepted Jesus into my life a year ago. I quit drinkin' and have tried to be a better man. It has taken me a year to get up the courage to find you and ask your forgiveness."

Laura hugged him and said, "Of course I forgive you. I was confused and hurt when you left, but mostly, I was concerned for you. But I thank God you've come back!"

Matthew started crying again as he said, "You have lifted a heavy weight from my heart."

Laura noticed he was shaking and coughing, and his color was not good. Daddy, you look tired. Let's go into the living room and let you stretch out on the sofa and rest."

"That's probably a good idea. I do feel a bit dizzy."

"I'll tell Odell to go on home. I'll call Miss Nellie Bell when you're ready to leave."

As Laura helped Matthew into the house, he noticed a large cat staring at him. "That's not Methuselah, is it?" said Matthew. Methuselah meowed.

Laura laughed, "Yes, it is. I think he recognizes you."

Once Laura had Matthew settled on the sofa, she went outside to talk to Odell.

"Odell, Mr. Matthew is ill. Go on and tell Miss Nellie Bell that he will stay the night here. I'll call her in the morning."

"Yes, ma'am," said Odell.

When Laura entered the living room, Matthew's eyes were closed. "Daddy, let me help you take your shoes off and stretch out, OK?"

Matthew complied and within minutes, was asleep.

Laura sat on a chair near him, watching him sleep. Childhood memories of her father played across her mind. How she loved him! His absence had been painful, and she thought she might never see him again.

"Thank you, Lord," said Laura, "for bringing my father back to me."

CHAPTER 60

THIS IS MY FATHER'S WORLD

After Odell informed Miss Nellie Bell of Matthew's illness, she immediately called her longtime physician, Dr. Barkley.

"Thomas? It's Nellie Bell. No, I'm fine. Healing nicely. I'm calling about someone else. Miss Helen's nephew, Matthew Layne, is ill and in need of a doctor. He is currently out at Sam and Laura Patterson's farm. He is Laura's father. Would it be possible for you to pay him a visit tomorrow morning? I'd be most grateful. Well, I'm not sure, but his color is bad, and he has a terrible cough and appears to be quite weak. Oh, wonderful! I'll have Odell pick you up at 7:30 tomorrow morning and drive you there. Thank you, Thomas."

Nellie Bell then called Laura, who picked up on the second ring, "Hello?"

"Laura, dear, it's Nellie Bell. Odell told me you would call in the morning, but you know me, I have to be on top of things. Did Matthew collapse?"

"No, but he is very weak, and his cough is bad. I had him lie down on the sofa, and he fell asleep almost immediately. He is exhausted. When he wakes up, I'll give him some aspirin and some hot tea with lemon and honey."

"That sounds perfect. And Laura, I hope you don't mind, but I have arranged for Odell to drive Dr. Barkley out to see Matthew. They will be there between 7:30 and 8:00 in the morning."

Laura felt just a twinge of resentment at Miss Nellie Bell's controlling nature, but knew it was a good idea.

"Thank you, Miss Nellie Bell. That is probably a good thing to do. I'll call you after Dr. Barkley leaves."

"And Laura, I'll send Matthew's belongings tomorrow with Odell. He has very little, but he might want it."

"Thank you. I'll call tomorrow, "said Laura.

Laura had just hung up the phone when she heard Hank's pickup truck wheels on the gravel. She walked outside to greet Sam.

"How is your wife doing, Hank?" asked Laura.

"Oh, she's OK. I think she's gettin' a lot of mileage out of that incident if you know what I mean," said Hank, laughing.

"Well, tell her hello for me," said Laura.

Sam put his arm around Laura's waist. "How was your day?"

"Sam. I've had quite a wonderful surprise. My father is here."

"What? Your father? He's alive?"

"Yes. Sam he found me and asked for my forgiveness. He's not feeling well, though. I insisted he lie on the sofa. He's asleep. Miss Nellie has arranged for her doctor to come here and see him tomorrow morning."

"I'm so happy for you, Laura. I know how much this means to you." They sat in the rockers and Laura poured both of them some lemonade.

"Any idea what he's been doing all these years?" asked Sam.

"No. It doesn't really matter. He might tell me one day, but the important thing is that he's alive, and he's here."

CHAPTER 61

THE GREAT PHYSICIAN

The next morning, at 7:50, they heard Odell and Dr. Barkley drive up and a car door slam. Laura went out to greet the doctor.

"Hello, Dr. Barkley, I'm Laura Patterson. Thanks so much for coming. I told my father you were coming, and he's not very happy about it. He claims he just needs to rest, but he still has a fever and a terrible cough."

Laura led the doctor into the living room, where Matthew was sitting up on the sofa.

"Mr. Layne, I understand you're not feeling well. Let's check you over, OK?" said the doctor.

"I'm fine, just kind of tired and developed a cough."

The doctor took out his stethoscope and listened to his chest. He checked his blood pressure and temperature.

"Mr. Layne, you have a terribly congested chest and a fever of 103 degrees. I want to take some x-rays of your chest, but I need to do this at the hospital."

"Is this really necessary? Can't I just take some aspirin and rest?" asked Matthew.

"We already tried that, Daddy. This is something more serious," said Laura.

"Laura," said the doctor, "can you come with us now to the hospital? Odell can drive all of us."

"Of course. Daddy, we need to do this, so please don't argue about it."

"All right, Laura, if you think this is necessary."

They all walked out to the porch where Odell had just unloaded Matthew's gear.

"Mr. Matthew, Miss Nellie Bell said to bring you your belongings in case you needed them. Miss Laura, should I put these inside?" asked Odell.

"Yes, thank you, Odell. And Odell, we'll need you to drop us all off at the hospital. Mr. Matthew needs some x-rays."

Later that afternoon, Dr. Barkley took Laura aside to talk with her privately.

"Laura, your father has pneumonia. He is also malnourished, dehydrated, and just plain old worn out. I suspect his liver is also affected from the excessive drinking. I want him to stay in the hospital for at least three days, maybe more. There are things we can do for him here that can't be done at home. If he improves, we may be able to send him home with you in a few days, but he will need a week or so of bedrest, and plenty of healthy food. Soups and broths are best. Hot tea with lemon and honey will soothe his cough."

"Will he eventually recover, doctor?"

"He will get better, but he will never be as strong as he once was. Laura, your father is only fifty-eight years old, but he has the body of someone much older. He cannot, under any circumstances, go back to living on the road like he was."

With tears in her eyes, Laura asked, "How long do you think he has?"

"If he goes back on the road and doesn't take care of himself, he won't last a year. With proper care and a change of lifestyle, he could live another five or six years. Some of that depends on his will to live, which, now that he has found you, seems strong."

"Thank you, doctor. I'm going to take good care of him. I just got him back. I can't lose him again."

CHAPTER 62

RETURN, O WANDERER

Matthew had been gone for five days. Sara Jane had hoped he would be back by now. She was helping Dolly gather eggs.

"Miss Dolly, I sure hope nothin' has happened to Mr. Matthew. It's been a long time."

"Not so long, really," said Dolly. "He said maybe four days, but he wasn't sure, and it's only one day past that. It seems longer because you miss him."

"You're right, Miss Dolly. I just need to have faith, don't I?"

"Yes, sweet girl. We all need to trust in the Lord. We also need to trust in Mr. Matthew. He's been on the road for years. He's a survivor. He knows how to take care of hisself. Before you know it, he'll be comin' up that road, a big ol' smile on his face." Dolly realized she was trying to convince herself as much as she was Sara Jane.

"I sure hope so, Miss Dolly, Mr. Matthew needs me and Buddy." Buddy gave a sharp bark. "Look! Buddy's hopin' you'll drop another egg," said Sara Jane. Buddy wagged his tail and smiled in agreement.

"Oops!" said Dolly, dropping another egg that Buddy quickly licked up.

Sara Jane laughed, "You dropped that on purpose, Miss Dolly!"

"Well, maybe I did, at that. We can't afford to break too many eggs, but one every now and then won't hurt."

They carried the eggs into the house and began cracking several open to prepare for supper.

"Miss Dolly, are they gonna be able to rebuild the school?"

"Soon as we can. Gonna take a while," said Dolly, washing some turnip greens.

"Did they catch the men that did that?"

"No, baby, they never will. Rumor has it that one of the deputies from the sheriff's office and his friends are all involved in that hateful KKK, and they sure ain't gonna arrest themselves."

"That just ain't right. Life sure ain't fair, is it Miss Dolly?"

"Sara Jane, I'm sure sorry you have to learn that at such an early age."

"But why does God allow such bad things to happen?"

"Oh, sweetie, the bad things don't come from God, they come from the devil. God gave us what's called "free will', which means we get to choose whether we want to be good or bad. Those folks that burned the school chose to be bad, but most folks choose to be good.
"

"But shouldn't God keep bad things from happenin' to good people?" asked Sara Jane.

"Baby, following Jesus don't mean bad things won't happen to us. It just means that He will walk with us and help us through the hard times. We'll never be alone if we have Jesus in our life."

Buddy followed Sara Jane as she took the purple hull peas out to the front porch to shell. "Buddy, I sure got a lot to learn about life."

CHAPTER 63

HELP SOMEBODY TODAY

Matthew slept through the afternoon after taking his medications. He was most unhappy to be in the hospital, but he hadn't complained too much for Laura's sake. She was sitting in a chair in his room when Sam walked in.

"Oh, Sam! I'm so glad you came. Let's go out into the waiting room."

"How's he doin'?" asked Sam.

"He's sleeping peacefully now. Dr. Barkley gave him a shot. He's got pneumonia. He's going to have to stay here a few days and have breathing treatments and take meds. If he improves enough, we can bring him home with us in a few days."

"I'm glad he was brought here. Sounds like he's sicker than we thought," said Sam.

"Oh, Sam. Dr. Barkley said he's in bad shape, and not just from the pneumonia. His liver and heart have been affected. Being on the road all these years has just broken him down. Dr. Barkley said if he goes back to that lifestyle untreated, he won't last a year. We have to help him, Sam."

Sam embraced Laura, who was softly crying. "Laura, of course we will. Your father can live with us if he'll agree to it."

"Oh, Sam! Thank you! Now, we just have to convince him that we want him with us. He's a proud man."

A nurse came into the waiting room. "Your father's awake and asking for you."

"Thank you. How is he doing?" asked Laura.

"His fever has gone down some, but he's still very weak. There's some soup and Jello, as well as some iced tea, on his bedside. You might want to help him," said the nurse.

When Laura and Sam walked into his room, Matthew's face lit up.

"Daddy, I'd like you to meet my husband, Sam. Sam, this is my father, Matthew."

Sam crossed to Matthew and shook his hand. "Nice to meet you, Mr. Layne."

"Nice to meet you, too, Sam."

"Daddy, let me help you eat some soup."

As she spooned the soup into Matthew's mouth, he coughed, spewing the soup everywhere.

"I'm so sorry, Laura. I made a mess."

"Just a little mess. Now let's try again." She continued to feed him, and thankfully, there were no more problems.

"Daddy, let's drink a little of this tea. There's also some Jello, if you feel like it."

"No Jello now, but the tea sounds good. I can hold the glass by myself."

There was a long pause as Matthew drank the tea, then he said, "I'm so sorry to be a burden. That's not why I came here."

"Mr. Layne, we don't see you as a burden. Your coming to see Laura is a blessing," said Sam.

Matthews' eyes filled with tears. "I'm grateful to you both."

"Mr. Layne, I'm going to take Laura home now. She's had a long day. But I'll make sure she gets back here tomorrow," said Sam.

"That's not necessary, Sam. I'm sure you both have things you need to do."

"Daddy, there's nothing more important than being here with you," said Laura.

Laura gave Matthew a kiss on the cheek and left the room with her husband.

After they left, Matthew said a prayer. "Thank you, Lord. I probably don't deserve your kindness to me, but I am so grateful to you for helping me find my daughter. I ask that you heal me, so I won't be a burden to her and her husband. Amen."

The nurse walked in and gave Matthew an injection of something to help the pain and help him sleep. He fell asleep five minutes later.

CHAPTER 64

GATHERING HOME

The following day, Laura returned to the hospital and found Matthew sitting up in bed. His color was better.

"Good morning, Daddy. You look like you feel a little better. I brought some of your things in case you needed them."

"Thank you, Laura. I feel a little better. The doctor said my fever is still at 101 degrees, but that's better than it was. I'm still coughin', but he said that was my body tryin' to rid itself of all that mess in my lungs."

"Do you mind if I open your rucksack? I want to take home any dirty clothes you might have and wash them along with the clothes you wore to the hospital," said Laura.

"That's OK. Don't have much in there, but my dirty clothes and a canteen."

Laura combed through the rucksack, pulling out the canteen and dirty clothes. She was about to close it when she noticed something wrapped in a towel. She unwrapped it and found a child's teacup. She immediately recognized it. Her eyes filled with tears.

"This is one of the teacups from the set Miss Helen gave me. Where did you find it?"

Matthew had forgotten about the teacup. Sara Jane must have wrapped it up and put it in her rucksack, hoping he would be able to give it to his daughter. Her kindness continued to touch his heart.

"When I went to our old house in Fort Worth, the woman who lives there now gave it to me. She said she had found it when they moved in."

Laura sat down, holding the tiny cup. "I'm so glad you saved it. I have such fond memories of tea parties with Ellen."

"Girls only," said Matthew.

"What?"

"I said, 'Girls only'. That's what you told me when I stuck my head inside your sheet tent tea party," said Matthew, smiling.

"That's right! I can't believe you remember that."

"May I keep this?" asked Laura.

"Of course. I'm glad it found its rightful owner." He paused, drinking some water. "Laura, I need to ask you to do one more thing for me. I was stayin' with a couple in Waco, Lewis and Dolly Carter. They are expectin' me to be back by now, and I don't want them to worry. I also want to make sure they are all OK. There were recent tornadoes in their area. They don't have a phone, but Lewis works at a small grocery and produce store in north Waco called James's Grocery and Produce. Will you ask Sam to call them later today and ask for Lewis?"

"Of course," said Laura. "By the way, Miss Nellie Bell is chomping at the bit to visit you, but Dr. Barkley told her to stay home."

Matthew smiled, "Probably a good idea."

"She said to tell you that you are in her prayers and that as soon as you get home, she's sending you some of Ezelle's chicken soup."

Laura left with Matthew's clothes, promising to return the next day. Matthew laid back down. He was exhausted. Laura had said, "As soon as you get home". Where exactly is home? And why hadn't he mentioned Sara Jane?

CHAPTER 65

OPEN MY EYES THAT I MAY SEE

When she got home, Laura asked Sam to call the Carter family at the store Matthew had mentioned. The operator placed his call.

"Hello? This is Sam Patterson. Is Lewis Carter there?"

"No sir, he's out at the produce stand. If you give me your number, I'll give it to him when he comes in," said the man.

"OK, thank you. Our number is 446-3402," said Sam, "Oh, tell him it's regarding Matthew Layne."

Laura and Sam had just sat down for supper when the phone rang. Sam got up and answered it.

"Hello?" said Sam.

"Hello, is this Sam Patterson?" asked Lewis.

"Yes, it is. How can I help you?' said Sam.

"Mr. Patterson, this is Lewis Carter. Did you call me?"

"Oh, yes, Mr. Carter. I'm Matthew Laynes's son-in-law. He is in the hospital in Rockdale and wanted to let you know he will be OK soon. He was afraid you might be worried about him. Also, he wanted to make sure you were all OK from the tornadoes."

"We had some damage to our house, but we're OK. We were worried about him, too. Do you have any idea when he might be comin' back? That's the first thing Sara Jane will want to know," said Lewis.

"I'm sorry, but who is Sara Jane? I thought your wife's name was Dolly," said Sam.

"Oh, I figured Mr. Matthew would have told you 'bout her. Sara Jane and her dog Buddy have been travelin' with him for a few weeks now. They've kind of been takin' care of each other," said Lewis.

Sam's heart started pounding. "Mr. Lewis, is Sara Jane, a girl around nine years old?"

"Yessir, that sounds about right. She gonna be so happy to hear Mr. Matthew is safe. I sure appreciate you callin', and I'll tell Dolly and Sara Jane as soon as I get home."

"Thank you, Mr. Carter. Oh, Matthew will be in the hospital for a few more days, then he will need to spend some time recovering at our house. I'll tell him to give you a call when he starts back your way."

"Thank you so much, Mr. Patterson. Goodbye."

Sam hung up the phone and stood there for a moment with a puzzled look on his face.

"Sam, what's this about a Sara Jane?" asked Laura.

"Laura, you're not gonna believe this, but I think we have found the missing girl."

"Oh, my goodness! You don't think it's the same Sara Jane? What on earth is she doing in Waco and at the same house as my father?"

"Mr. Carter confirmed she's around nine years old and has been traveling with your father for a few weeks. It's got to be her, but how on earth did those two end up together?"

"I'll talk to Daddy in the morning, and we'll figure it all out. This is all so strange. What if it really is her? Should we call Sheriff Black?"

"Not until we speak with your father and get more information," said Sam.

As they lay in bed that night, Laura said, "Sam, you don't think my father's in some kind of trouble, do you?"

"I sure hope not," said Sam.

Neither one slept well that night.

CHAPTER 66

THE FOUNDLING

Sam told Hank he needed to take the morning off to meet with Laura's father. He and Laura drove to the hospital early the next morning. They were full of questions and anxiety.

When they entered the room, the nurse was helping Matthew sit up so he could take his meds.

"Good morning, Daddy? How are you feeling?" asked Laura.

"Getting a little stronger each day, thanks to you," said Mattthew.

Sam sat in the chair as Laura sat on the side of the hospital bed.

"Daddy, Sam made that call to Mr. Lewis for you. He was so happy to hear from you. He said they had some damage to their house, but they were unhurt. He said someone named Sara Jane would be so relieved. Who is Sara Jane?"

Matthew paused, confused at first, then realized he had never mentioned her to them. "Sara Jane is the little girl I've been lookin' after. She lost her parents a while back, and her house burned down with her stepfather inside. I met her in Rockdale the day I was leavin'. She had nobody and nowhere to go and asked me if she could ride in the boxcar with me. She seemed to sense I was harmless, as did her dog. I agreed because I was afraid she might be harmed travelin' by herself. The three of us became fast friends and have been travelin' together for several weeks now."

"The three of you?" asked Sam.

"Yes. Her, me, and her dog Buddy."

There was a long pause, then Laura said, "Daddy, everybody's been lookin' for her. Nobody knew what happened to her. The sheriff has bulletins everywhere, even in neighboring counties. There are even bulletins at train stations."

Matthew turned pale. "I had no idea people were searchin' for her."

"How did you end up at the Carter's house?" asked Sam.

"Some bulls hired by the railroad made us get off the train near Waco. We had to sleep outdoors, and Sara, Jane and Buddy were attacked by a bobcat and terribly injured. Lewis took us to his home in his truck. His wife Dolly nursed Sara Jane and Buddy back to health. Once they were stabilized, I headed to Milam County to try and find you, Laura. I promised Sara Jane I would come back for her, and I still plan to do that."

"But what were you planning to do once you went back for her, continue staying with the Carters?" asked Sam.

"I hadn't worked it all out yet. I was hopefully gonna find some work and find a place where I could make a home for her. She needs stability and protection."

"Daddy, we need to let the sheriff know where she is so he can stop looking for her," said Laura.

"No! Don't do that, not until I'm with her. She'll be scared to death if some sheriff shows up and takes her away. It might also cause a problem for the Carters."

"So what do you suggest we do, Mr. Layne?" asked Sam.

"Look, I understand that the sheriff should know, but don't tell him where she is or any of the circumstances yet. Promise to explain everything in a couple of weeks. That way, we could all go to Waco and bring her back with us. She won't be scared that way. Please don't just turn her over to the law. She deserves better," said Matthew.

"Sam, that sounds like a good compromise. We need to protect her as long as we can," said Laura.

"OK, do you want to tell the sheriff, or should I?" said Sam.

"I should. I'm the one he's been talking to," said Laura.

"Promise you won't tell anyone else, especially Nellie Bell. Her curiosity could cause problems," said Matthew.

"I hate to keep her in the dark, but I understand," said Laura.

"Daddy, we're going to the sheriff's office and tell him only what you asked us to, OK. Do you need anything before we go?"

"No, thank you. And thank you for helpin' me protect Sara Jane. She's a wonderful little girl, and she's been through so much. I just don't want her to go through more trauma."

CHAPTER 67

I'VE FOUND A FRIEND

Thirty minutes later, Sam and Laura arrived at Sheriff Grady Black's office in Cameron.

"Laura, what a surprise! And this is your husband?" said the sheriff.

"Yes, this is my husband, Sam."

As they shook hands, the sheriff said, "Please have a seat. How can I help you?"

Laura looked at Sam, then jumped right in.

"Sheriff Black, we have something to tell you, but we need your promise that it won't be repeated outside this office," said Laura.

"I guess I need to hear what you have to say first," said the sheriff.

"I'll just have to trust you then. We have reliable information as to the whereabouts of Sara Jane Evans," said Laura.

"Where is she?" asked the sheriff.

"I can't tell you that. You have to trust me, like I am trusting you. All I can tell you is that we know where she is and that she is safe and unharmed. If you will bear with us, we will have her back in Rockdale and will explain everything within the next two weeks."

Sheriff Black was stunned. He said, "Wow! That's a lot to digest. And you sure you won't tell me where she is?"

"I'm sorry, sheriff, but I just can't do that. I promise you will understand when you find out why," said Laura.

The sheriff paused, then said, "Well, I guess I'll just have to trust you then."

They all stood up, then Laura said, "And remember. Tell no one."

Sam added, "Thank you, Sheriff Black. You won't regret this."

After they left, the sheriff sat back down at his desk. What in the world was going on? He hoped he wasn't making a mistake trusting the Pattersons.

As they were driving home, Laura said, "Thank you, Sam, for going along with that. After listening to my father, I'm sure we did the right thing." There was a long pause, then Laura continued, "Sam, do you think Sara Jane could live with us, too? I know it's a lot to ask, but…"

"Of course, she can. She and your father have bonded. I think she would be happy living with us, especially since he'll be there, too."

"If he'll agree. You know, if he knows she'll be with us, I'll bet he'll agree to stay. And thank you, Sam, for agreeing to let her live with us. If you weren't driving, I'd kiss you all over!"

"Want me to pull over?" said Sam, with a twinkle in his eye.

Laura laughed and moved over closer to Sam.

THE GOOD NEWS

When Lewis arrived home that evening, Buddy was lying on the newly screened-in porch. A tarp covered the damaged part of the roof, and a screen covered the windows instead of glass. All in good time, thought Lewis, all in good time. He was grateful that winter was still months away, giving him time to install glass in the windows. The roof repair would have to wait.

Buddy barked a greeting and wagged his tail at Lewis as he walked into the kitchen, where Dolly and Sara Jane were preparing supper.

"Hey! Anybody wanna hear some good news?" said Lewis as he entered the kitchen, a big smile on his face. He lifted the lid of a pot and said, "Somethin' sho smell good in here!"

"What's got into you, Lewis?" asked Dolly.

"What got into me is some good news!" He attempted to swing Dolly around, no easy task even on the best of days. "I got a phone call from Mr. Matthew's son-in-law. He say Mr. Matthew is in the hospital in Rockdale, but he gonna be OK. He has to stay there for a few more days, then they will take him home and let him recover. He say Mr. Matthew want to make sure we was all OK after that tornado. Also, he say he didn't want us to think he wasn't comin' back. He gonna be back in about a week or so. He gonna call the store when he's headed this way."

"Oh, Mr. Lewis, thank you! That's great news. I was so worried about him. I gotta go tell Buddy the good news."

As Sara Jane ran out of the kitchen, Dolly called, "Now, don't be long, sweet girl, we about to eat."

Dolly and Lewis sat at the table, Lewis finally remembering to remove his hat.

"Lewis, that sure is good news. But I been thinkin', what are Mr. Matthew and Sara Jane gonna do when he gets back? Where they gonna live? That child don't need to be ridin' the rails all over the country, and he don't neither."

"I don't know, Dolly. All we can do is turn it over to the Lord to make a way where there don't seem to be one."

CHAPTER 69

BLEST BE THE TIE

Matthew continued to improve daily, and after being in the hospital four more days, was able to move to the Patterson farm.

"Daddy, we fixed up the first-floor bedroom for you. Your things are in there."

"Thank you, Laura. Is it OK if I sit on the porch for a while? I missed the fresh air."

"Of course it is. I'll bring you some lemonade," said Laura, crossing into the kitchen.

Suddenly, Methuselah jumped into Matthew's lap, startling him.

"Whoa! So, you remember me, do you, Methuselah?"

Methuselah purred loudly as Matthew stroked his fur.

"It's good to see you, too. We're both a little worse for the wear, but we're still above ground," said Matthew.

Queenie came onto the porch and lay down next to Matthew's rocker.

"Well, hello, dog. What's your name?"

Laura, just walking onto the porch with the lemonade, said, "That's Queenie. Sam gave her to me for my last birthday. You won't hear her bark; she has something wrong with her voice box. She is such a sweet dog."

"Well, I sure feel popular. I ain't had this much attention in years," said Matthew, smiling. "That husband of yours sure seems like a good fella. Where did you meet him?"

Smiling, Laura said, "Remember my friend, Susan, who lived on our street? Well, Susan was dating a boy named Lowell, who went to our school. Sam is Lowell's cousin and lives in Dallas. Anyway, Sam was visiting Lowell one day, and Susan asked if I would double date with her and Lowell. Well, Lowell was a nice guy, so I figured his cousin might be, too. Turns out I was right. Sam started making lots more trips to visit his cousin, and six months later, we were married."

"Six months, huh?" said Matthew.

"Daddy, when you know, you know."

"I like that story," said Matthew.

They heard Hank's pickup drive up. Sam got out and walked toward the front porch, smiling. "My ears are burning. Ya'll aren't talking about me, are you?"

Laura rose and gave Sam a hug. "As a matter of fact, we are. Daddy said you seem like a good fella, and I agreed. Sit down, Sam. I'll bring you some lemonade."

"It's good to see you home, Mr. Layne. How are you feeling?"

"Much better. I figure a few more days of rest, and I'll be good as new."

Laura handed Sam his lemonade and sat on a bench nearby. She gave Sam a knowing look, and he gave her a little nod in response.

"Mr. Layne, Laura and I want to talk to you about something. We would like it if you would live with us indefinitely."

"Indefinitely? Oh, I don't know what to say. That's not why I came here. I hadn't planned on interruptin' your lives or bein' a burden."

"You're not a burden, Mr. Layne. You're a blessing. We really want you to live with us," said Sam.

"That's mighty nice of you, Sam. But can you give me a little time to think about it? I hadn't expected this."

"You take all the time you want. But while you're thinking, let me sweeten the pot a little. We would also like Sara Jane to live with us," said Sam.

"Sara Jane? You would be willin' to take her in, too?"

"Yes, Daddy. "We would like to give both of you a home with us," said Laura.

Matthew's eyes filled with tears, "I don't know what I ever did to deserve you, Laura. I thank God for you and Sam every day."

"Is that a 'yes', Mr. Layne?" said Sam.

Matthew said, "It's a 'yes' for Sara Jane, and a 'maybe' for me. I'll talk to her when I get to Waco and make sure it's OK with her."

"When _we_ get to Waco, Daddy. Sam is going to drive us."

"I don't know what to say," said Matthew. "Thank you both."

Three days later, Matthew said he was feeling better and was anxious to get to Waco. He claimed it was Ezelle's chicken soup that had done the trick.

"When can we go get Sara Jane?" asked Matthew.

"I'm thinking this Saturday will be good. We could leave around 10:00 that morning, have lunch and a visit, and then be back way before dark. Will that give you enough time to get Sara Jane's room ready?" asked Sam.

"Yes," said Laura, smiling, "I've already started working on it."

"I'll call Lewis at the store and tell him we'll be there in two days," said Sam.

"Thank you, Sam. I can't wait for you to meet Sara Jane. She's a very special child. By the way, I hope it's OK to bring her dog, Buddy, back, too. She won't come without him," said Matthew.

"No problem," said Sam, "he can hang out with Queenie."

"I think he already has," said Laura, smiling.

CHAPTER 70

MR. MATTHEW IS COMING

When Lewis got home with the news, Sara Jane jumped up and down.

"He's comin', Buddy! Mr. Matthew is comin' back to us!"

Buddy wagged his tail and gave a bark as though he understood.

"Sara Jane," said Dolly, "we need to clean the house a little, and I'll need your help makin' a nice lunch for them on Saturday. Mr. Matthew's son-in-law and daughter are comin', too. They are anxious to meet you and Buddy."

"Oh! I'll get to meet his daughter! That is so nice. Miss Dolly, can I please wear my church dress you made me?"

"Of course, you can."

"I'll go get the broom," said Sara Jane.

Lewis and Dolly laughed, then Dolly became serious. "Lewis, what do you think's gonna happen? They gonna leave them here or take them back with them?"

"Don't know for sure. We'll just have to see."

"I'm sure gonna miss them if they leave," said Dolly. "I love that child like she's my own."

"I know. Me and Mr. Matthew became good friends. He was a big help to me at work. House gonna feel real empty," said Lewis.

CHAPTER 71

TOGETHER AGAIN

The big day was here. Dolly and Sara Jane were busily preparing a nice lunch of fried chicken, collard greens, black-eyed peas, and sliced tomatoes, courtesy of the produce stand at Mr. James's store and their own garden. Dolly was an excellent cook and had taught Sara Jane quite a bit to add to her rudimentary skills.

Around 11:30 AM, they heard a car drive up, and Buddy started barking.

"It's them! It's them!" cried Sara Jane, yanking her apron off and running outside. Buddy ran outside to help her greet Mr. Matthew. When he climbed out of the car's passenger seat, she ran to him and embraced him. "You're here! You're here! You said you'd come back for me, and you did!"

Matthew teared up. He felt he had been away for months instead of weeks. "Sara Jane, there are a couple of people I want you to meet. Laura, this is Sara Jane. Sara Jane, please meet my daughter, Laura Patterson."

Sara Jane's mouth dropped open." It's you! Miss Laura is your daughter?"

"Yes, I am proud to say she is."

"But I... I didn't know. Miss Laura, it was me and Buddy that stayed in your barn. You were so nice to us."

"I didn't know who it was, Sara Jane. I figured it out later. I am so happy to see that you are safe. We were worried about you. Oh, this is my husband, Sam."

"Nice to meet you, Mr. Sam. Did your friend ever get that squeaky pickup door fixed?"

Sam and Laura laughed.

"As a matter of fact, he did. It's a funny story. I'll tell you sometime."

Lewis and Dolly came out into the yard.

"Laura and Sam, meet Dolly and Lewis Carter, our guardian angels. Lewis and Dolly, please meet my daughter Laura and her husband, Sam."

"We are so happy to meet you," said Laura. "We've heard wonderful things about you. Thank you so much for taking care of my father and Sara Jane."

"It was our pleasure," said Dolly. "We've come to love both of them. Sara Jane been a big help to me while you were gone, Mr. Matthew."

"I'm glad to hear it," said Matthew.

"Well, y'all come on in. Dolly and Sara Jane done fixed a nice lunch for us," said Lewis. "The kitchen's a little small, so we set up here on the front porch. Just got it re-screened after the tornado."

"I'm so glad y'all are OK. I was worried," said Matthew.

"And we was worried about you, too," said Lewis.

"Praise the Lord, we are all safe," said Dolly.

"Sam, will you and Daddy get the food out of the trunk?"

"Of course," said Sam.

"Miss Laura, you and Sara Jane, come on in and sit down. Buddy, you gonna have to stay out here for now., but you gonna have some good eatin' later," said Dolly.

Lewis had helped Dolly pull the kitchen table out to the porch. Then he'd added a large board on top of two sawhorses. They had added tablecloths and set the table. The food had been brought in and already set on the table. Sara Jane had picked some wildflowers and put them in a mason jar, which sat in the middle of the table. Glasses of iced tea stood by each plate.

"This is so nice, Dolly," said Laura.

"Thank you. Sara Jane helped me fix all of it."

"That's wonderful, Sara Jane," said Laura, as Sara Jane beamed.

Sam and Matthew entered the porch and set a large smoked ham and a dewberry cobbler on the table.

"My goodness!" said Dolly. "What's all this?"

"We brought you a ham, and Laura made you her special dewberry cobbler," said Matthew.

"That's my favorite!" said Sara Jane. "My other favorite is peach."

After everyone was seated, Lewis asked everyone to bow their heads for the blessing.

"Dear Lord, we ask you to bless this food to the nourishment of our bodies. We give thanks for the safe return of Mr. Matthew. We also thank you for our new friends, the Pattersons, and wish them a safe journey home. Amen.”

After lunch, Sam said, “Dolly, that was the best fried chicken I ever had.” He got a look from Laura, then added, “Except for my wife’s, of course.” They all laughed.

After Dolly, Sara Jane, and Laura cleared the table, Matthew asked.

Sara Jane to go for a walk. Buddy tagged along. They walked until they came to a short wall that was shaded by a tree.

“Sara Jane, I need to talk to you about somethin’.”

Sara Jane’s heart sank. “You’re not gonna go away again, are you, Mr. Matthew?”

“Not exactly, at least not by myself. Sara Jane, my daughter and her husband have invited us to come live with them.”

“Both of us? In that big farmhouse?”

“Yes.”

“Can Buddy come, too?”

“I already asked them, and they said yes.”

Sara Jane hugged Matthew’s neck. With tears in her eyes, she said, “Oh, Mr. Matthew. This is so wonderful! We’ll all be together in that big, beautiful house! We’re gonna be a family!”

While Matthew and Sara Jane were on their walk, Laura and Sam spoke with Lewis and Dolly.

“We sure thank you for all you’ve done for Matthew and Sara Jane. I understand you also nursed Buddy back to health. As you know, Matthew has been on the road for the last eight years. His health has been seriously affected. The doctor says if he goes back to that lifestyle, he won't last a year," said Sam.

"Oh, no!" said Dolly.

Laura spoke up, "The good news is that we have invited my father to live with us. With proper rest and good food, he can live several more years. We would also like Sara Jane to live with us. We've got plenty of room. My father is speaking with her now. We wanted to tell you privately because we know how close you've grown to Sara Jane and she to you."

"Miss Laura, that is wonderful news. We didn't know what was gonna happen after you came here today. I'll sure miss that sweet girl, but I'm so happy she'll have a home with the three of you."

"Thank you, Dolly. We told my father to tell Sara Jane that we'll come for a visit during the Christmas season and summer break if that's alright with you."

Dolly teared up and said, "Oh, thank you, Miss Laura. That would mean so much to us."

Matthew, Sara Jane, and Buddy returned from their walk. Laura noticed that both had a big smile on their faces. In fact, was it her imagination, or was the dog smiling, as well?

Matthew said, "Well, Sara Jane has agreed to come live with us."

Sara Jane ran to Laura and hugged her neck. "Thank you, thank you!"

Laura teared up as she hugged Sara Jane.

"Well, Miss Sara Jane, we better gather up your things. We're sure gonna miss you, baby girl."

"Mr. Matthew said we can come for visits twice a year. And I'll write to you, OK? Will you please write me back? I'm gonna miss you so much," said Sara Jane as she hugged Dolly and Lewis.

"Of course I will. Now, let's get your things."

They all walked out to the car. Matthew shook hands with Lewis and gave Dolly a hug.

"Lewis, Dolly, I'll never forget your kindness. We'll see you in December."

They both wished Matthew well, then walked back into the house, the screened door slamming behind them.

CHAPTER 72

HOME SWEET HOME

It was almost dark by the time they made it back to the Patterson farm. Sara Jane's eyes lit up when she saw the beautiful house and realized she would get to live in it. Buddy jumped out of the car and ran to the front porch to greet Queenie, who licked his face and wagged her tail. Methuselah remained in his spot, reserving judgment.

When they walked into the house, Laura said, "Let me give you a tour, Sara Jane. Your room is upstairs, down the hall from ours. Mr. Matthew's room is on this floor."

After touring the downstairs (some of which Sara Jane had seen before), they went upstairs to see Sara Jane's room. Sara Jane's eyes grew wide as she stared at the most beautiful room she had ever seen. It was painted ocean blue and had a mermaid painted on one wall, and a sea turtle and a starfish painted on another. Above her bed was a fishing net decorated with seashells.

"How did you know I loved the ocean?" asked Sara Jane.

"My father told us about your special seashell from your father and how you want to go to the ocean one day."

Sara Jane sat on her new bed and looked around. "I feel like a fairy princess in this room. Thank you so much, Miss Laura." Tears trickled down her cheeks.

"You are most welcome. We feel blessed to have you with us, Sara Jane." She took Sara Jane's hand in hers, tears in her eyes.

While Laura and Sara Jane were upstairs, Matthew and Sam were sitting on the front porch.

"Sam, I thank you again for givin' a home to that sweet girl. I didn't know how I was gonna take care of her. This is a wonderful solution."

"We are happy to have both of you, Mr. Layne. There's something you should know. Last fall, Laura lost our baby girl. We named her Emily after her mother. Having a child in the house will really lift her spirits."

"I'm so very sorry. I had no idea," said Matthew.

"She doesn't talk about it much. It's just too painful. Family is everything to her, Mr. Layne. Having Sara Jane and you here is a real blessing."

Matthew didn't speak, afraid his voice might crack.

Sara Jane came bounding down the stairs and out onto the porch,

"Mr. Matthew, have you seen my room? It is the most beautiful room I ever saw! Thank you for telling Miss Laura about my seashell."

"You're welcome. I'm glad you like your room."

Sara Jane whispered to Matthew, "Mr. Matthew, do you think they'd let me have Buddy in my room?"

“I already checked. They said OK.”

“Buddy, did you hear that! You can sleep in my room! Come see it. It’s beautiful!”

“That child is full of joy and gratitude,” said Sam.

“She’s not the only one,” said Matthew.

CHAPTER 73

RETURN, O WANDERER

Monday morning, Sheriff Grady Black was sitting at his desk looking over some papers when the phone rang.

"Sheriff Black here."

"Grady? It's Nellie Bell. I need you to come to my house in one hour."

"Is something wrong?"

"No. Something is very right. There is someone I want you to meet."

"Nellie Bell, I really don't have time for a social call. I've got a lot on my plate today." Was this another "lovely girl" she wanted him to meet?

"Grady, this is important. You'll thank me for it. I'll expect you at 10 AM sharp." She hung up. There was no telling Nellie Bell "no".

At 10 AM sharp, Grady knocked on her door. He wondered who owned the car parked out front. And since when did Nellie Bell own a dog? Ezelle opened the door and greeted him.

"Good mornin', Sheriff Black. Please come in. Miss Nellie Bell is expectin' you."

She led him into the parlor. Nellie Bell reclined on her chaise lounge as usual. A large silver coffee service and several cups sat on a table, along with Ezell's famous oatmeal cookies on a silver tray. And there was cake. Chocolate cake. His favorite. What on earth was going on?

"Sit down, Grady. You'll be glad you accepted my invitation," said Nellie Bell.

"Don't you mean your summons?" said the sheriff, removing his Stetson.

Ignoring him, Nellie Bell said, "Ezelle, will you bring in our guests, please?"

Ezelle walked to the library where the "guests" were waiting and led them into the parlor.

Nellie Bell rose unsteadily and said, "Sheriff Grady Black, I'd like you to meet Miss Sara Jane Evans. Sara Jane, this is Sheriff Grady Black."

The sheriff was stunned. "Hello, there, young lady. Nice to meet you at last." He stuck out his hand.

"Hello, Sheriff Black," said Sara Jane, "You ain't gonna arrest me, are you?"

They all laughed. Only Sara remained serious.

"No, I hadn't planned to. Do you want me to?" said the sheriff.

"No, sir. I surely do not want you to, but I was afraid you might."

"Let's all sit down, shall we?" said Nellie Bell. "Grady, I believe you know Laura and Sam Patterson. And this is Laura's father, Matthew Layne, Sara Jane's traveling companion."

Matthew leaned over to shake the sheriff's hand.

"Ezelle, will you serve the coffee, please? And please take Sara Jane into the kitchen for lemonade and cookies," said Nellie Bell.

After Ezelle and Sara Jane left the room, Nellie Bell said, "I'm sure you are wondering what's going on, Grady. We will all do our best to explain. Laura, dear, would you like to go first?" said Nellie Bell.

"Sheriff Black, Sam and I appreciate your patience. My father came to my house a couple of weeks ago. I had not seen him for eight years, and presumed he was dead. He became ill and spent time in the hospital. At his request, my husband made a call to a home in Waco where he had been staying. He wanted to let them know he was OK and would return as soon as he was well. Sam, will you continue?"

"When I spoke to Lewis Carter, the friend Mr. Layne asked me to call, he mentioned that 'Sara Jane' would be so happy to hear Mr. Layne was safe. He confirmed that the girl was around nine years of age. Laura and I immediately thought of Sara Jane Evans but were completely confused as to how it could possibly be the same girl," said Sam.

"After speaking with my father the next morning, we confirmed it was the same Sara Jane. We were going to report it to you, Sheriff Black, but my father convinced us not to," said Laura.

Matthew spoke up. "I explained that Sara Jane had been through so much tragedy. More than you know. She was frightened and homeless and had finally found shelter with the Carter's in Waco. A sheriff showing up at the Carter's house to take her away would traumatize her and cause problems for the Carters. I begged them to please wait until we could go pick her up and bring her to Rockdale."

"So, you see, Sheriff Black. That's why we couldn't tell you her location. I appreciate your trusting us," said Laura.

"But how on earth do you all know each other?" said the sheriff.

"I'll answer that," said Nellie Bell. "Matthew is my dear friend Helen's nephew, and he is Laura's father, as you heard earlier. I've known both of them their entire lives. Helen always brought them by when they visited her from Fort Worth. I once met Sara Jane when she was around five years old, and her sweet parents helped me load and unload groceries. That is my only connection to her."

"So, we're talkin' about a whole bunch of puzzle pieces finally comin' together. Serendipity," said the sheriff.

"God," said Laura. "Only God could bring us all together like this."

"You may be right, Laura," said the sheriff.

"I do have a question for you, Mr. Layne," said the sheriff. "How did you and Sara Jane know each other?"

"We didn't. I met her for the first time in Rockdale. She told me she had lost her parents and her home and had nowhere to go. She asked to ride along with me. I agreed because I knew she needed protection from all the evil out there."

"Wow. I'm glad she met you. It could have turned out bad. I may have some more questions for you later, but that's all for now."

"Ezelle, will you bring Sara Jane into the parlor, please?" said Nellie Bell.

"Yes'm," said Ezelle, escorting Sara Jane back into the room.

"I do have a couple of questions for you, Sara Jane," said the sheriff.

"Grady, now is not the time. You can speak with Sara Jane another time. She's not going anywhere. Right now we have some celebrating to do. Help yourselves to cookies and cake, everyone," said Nellie Bell.

Sheriff Grady looked at the happy, chatting group. As he ate his favorite cake, he realized that he would have one heck of a report to write up. He was so relieved the girl was safe and he could close the case. Never in a million years would he have figured this out on his own. How it had all come together was nothing short of miraculous. Did he believe in miracles? He did now.

EPILOGUE

SIX DAYS LATER

The following Sunday, Sara Jane twirled in front of the mirror in her new dress and shoes. She had never had a 'store-bought' dress before. She felt like a princess.

"What do you think, Buddy?"

Buddy wagged his tail and gave a quick bark of appreciation.

Sara Jane was excited to go back to her home church. Her stepfather had prevented her from attending since her mother died, and she had missed it.

The week she had been with the Pattersons had been wonderful. The first morning there, she had awakened, thinking it had all been a dream. When she realized it was real, she said a prayer of gratitude.

At her request, the Pattersons and Matthew had taken her back to the site of her burned house. She stood staring at it for a long time as though she needed to process the reality of it. She needed to relive the horror so she could heal and move on.

After the bad memories, however, came the good ones. She had such good memories of her years with her mother and father and all the love they had shared.

The Pattersons walked with her to her tree house, where she retrieved her precious jar of peaches. As she held the jar, she felt her mother's presence. They smiled when she told them about the day in the peach orchard she had shared with her mother. Laura noticed the peaches were just starting to ripen and promised to bring Sara Jane back in a couple of weeks to pick some. Sara Jane told her that Dolly had taught her how to make peach cobbler, and she would make some for all of them.

Their last step had been to the church cemetery, where she and Laura had placed wildflowers on the graves of Sara Jane's mother, father, and baby brother. They then crossed to the graves of Miss Helen and baby Emily, where Matthew was standing, his hat in his hands, and tears in his eyes. They let him place the flowers. It had been a meaningful, yet emotional day.

Laura's voice brought Sara Jane back to reality. "Sara Jane, are you ready?"

"Yes, ma'am, comin'!"

Sara Jane bounded down the stairs, Buddy following in excitement. They loaded into the car and drove to Sandy Creek Methodist Church, where they were warmly greeted by Pastor Chris and the members of the congregation. Sara Jane's old friend, Amy, whom she had not seen since her mother died, hugged her and promised to plan a tea party soon.

As they sat in their usual spot, the third pew "congregation right", Pastor Chris said a prayer of thanksgiving for the safe return of Sara Jane, then asked them all to stand and sing Laura's favorite hymn, "Standing on the Promises."

As they sang, Laura noticed how the sunlight streamed in from Miss Helen's beautiful stained glass windows, the colors playing over the faces of her family. She could feel Miss Helen smiling down. With tears in her eyes and her heart overflowing with love and gratitude, Laura looked up and said, "I know it was you, God."

RESOURCES

The following hymns mentioned in the book can be found in Hymnary.org. All but "Standing on the Promises" are also in The Cokesbury Worship Hymnal , C.A. Bowen, D.D., The Methodist Publishing House, 1938.

Beautiful River, Robert Lowry
Blest Be the Tie, John Fawcett and Hans Gnaeli
Bringing in the Sheaves, Knowles Shaw and George A. Minor
Down by the Riverside, AfricanAmerican Spiritual
Gathering Home, Mary B.C. Slade and Rigdon McCoy McIntosh
Help Somebody Today, Carrie Elizabeth Ellis Breck and Charles Hutchinson Gabriel
Higher Ground, Johnson Oatman, Jr.
I've Found a Friend, James G. Small and George C. Stebbins
Oh, Brother Man, John G. Whittier and J.W. Lerman
O, Happy Day, Philip Doddridge and E. F. Rimbau
Standing on the Promises, Russell Kelso Carter
Steal Away, Old Slave Song
The Great Physician, William Hunter and John H. Stockton
There's a Wideness in God's Mercy, Frederick W. Faber and Lizzie s. Tourjee
This is my Father's World, Maltbic D. Babcock
We've a Story to Tell, Collin Sterne and H.E. Nichol

Thank you for reading my book! Stay tuned for my next book, WHILE THE WORLD REJOICES, a sequel to STANDING ON THE PROMISES, due out in winter 2024.

I can be reached at:
Facebook author page: Beverly Daniel, Author
Email: Writingbybeverly@gmail.com

Author Bio:

Beverly Daniel is a writer, actress, and retired English and theatre arts teacher. She has written and illustrated three children's books, as well as numerous skits and short plays. She currently lives in the Dallas, Texas area with her husband Mark and their rescue cat and rescue dog.

Other books by Beverly Daniel available Fall 2024